THE COMPLETE AIR FRYER COOKBOOK

THE COMPLETE AIR FRYER COOKBOOK

Over 100 easy, energy-efficient recipes for every meal

CONTENTS

6 SUPER EASY GUIDE
TO AIR FRYERS

12 HEALTHIER
SNACKS

44 FAVOURITE
DINNERS

90 VEGGIES
& SIDES

128 WEEKENDS

174 AIR BAKE

220 CONVERSION CHART

221 INDEX

SUPER EASY GUIDE TO AIR FRYERS

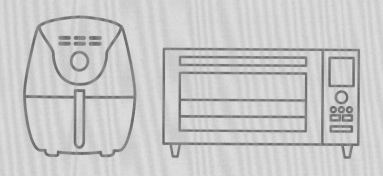

HOW THEY WORK

The air fryer is renowned for replicating the crisp texture of deep-fried foods using a fraction of the oil. This amped-up worktop convection oven works by pushing hot air around food; the rapid circulation of air in the confined space helps to make food crisp, just like deep-frying but with much less oil. For example, air-fried hot chips contain just 4–6g fat versus 17g for the deep-fried equivalent.

THE DIFFERENT TYPES OF AIR FRYERS

There are many different sizes and shapes of air fryer available, from compact spaceship-looking styles, which sit upright and have a deep pull-out drawer, to air fryers that look like mini ovens. These are also designed to sit on a worktop, but they are less compact and more comparable in size to a microwave oven.

BASKET AIR FRYERS These compact versions range in capacity from 3–4 litres to 6–7 litres and are typically the more affordable option. With this style, the base of the handled basket is perforated and slightly elevated above the bottom of the pan, which collects oil drippings and cooking juices. While they are nifty, they do not allow for large volumes of food, and you will not be able to cook an entire family meal in them.

OVEN AIR FRYERS These larger versions of air fryers (11 litres) open like an oven with a door. They offer the convenience of a compact oven with the benefits of an air fryer, and for a single person or couple could even suffice as their only cooking medium. These appliances come equipped with two or three wire racks for shelves, which allow for a variety of foods being cooked at the same time. They also include additional functions, such as a low-temperature mode for dehydrating and a defrost mode for thawing food. As well, they come with preset functions for cooking foods such as chips and fries, chops, prawns (shrimp), chicken drumsticks and steaks. The clear oven door allows you to see how the cooking is progressing without the need to open it, keeping the temperature stable inside. Naturally, with these additional benefits, the price tag for these larger appliances is higher, ranging from the low hundreds upwards. For this book we've used popular well-priced and mid-sized 5.3-litre and 7-litre models. We have also used the dehydrator function of a larger 11-litre three-in-one air fryer. If you have a larger appliance, you will be able to cook larger amounts of food, while for a smaller one you will need to decrease quantities accordingly to fit in your appliance.

SAFETY

Before using your air fryer, carefully read the manufacturer's instructions for your appliance.

Air fryers can get hot, so allow sufficient space on the worktop around it. The vent at the back extracts steam, and with it grease, so you will find that you need to wipe down the surface behind your air fryer.

Once the basket is pulled out of the appliance, treat it as if it has come out of the oven – it will be hot! Take care when adding and removing items from the air-fryer basket.

It is also important to clean your appliance after every use, both the inner basket and the outer pan, to remove grease, as otherwise the appliance will smoke and any small trapped pieces of food will burn.

FRYING

Air fryers excel at crisping dry ingredients, but where they don't work well is for foods with wet batters – the batter will simply stick rather than get crispy. It is also not just a case of popping food into the air fryer instead of into hot oil in a pan. The cooking method needs to be adapted to create a comparable result.

THE OTHER STUFF

The air fryer is far more than a single-use appliance for making crunchy, crispy chips. For starters, it helps to think past the name, which is a bit of a misnomer. The appliance is not a deep fryer at all and actually offers many of the benefits an oven does.

Its major limitation is the interior capacity; be sure that the dish or dishes you plan to use in your air fryer are heatproof and will fit in the appliance with room for air to circulate. Avoid any that are too tall and will come in contact with the top element of the appliance; otherwise the food will burn.

If you are using the appliance to bake, avoid very light-textured or liquidy batters, as the vortex created by the appliance is strong enough to make the batter spit or create a volcanic-looking top on your baked item.

Keep an eye on sugary mixtures, as in an air fryer browning will be accelerated.

5 BEST FOODS TO COOK IN THE AIR FRYER

ACCESSORIES

Racks Most basket-style air fryers come equipped with at least one basic circular rack. Also useful is a toast rack to assist with bread slices sitting upright.

Tins Investing in cake tins that fit in your appliance will enable you to get the most out of it. Many small conventional tins will fit. Muffin tins for standard ovens won't, so buy a circular tray with muffin inserts.

Utensils While most everyday kitchen utensils such as tongs, spatulas and lifters can be used in the air fryer, it is worth investing in ones with silicone ends, if you want to maintain the protective surface of your appliance.

Small silicone mats
Small silicone mats are perfect for lining the bottom of the air fryer when cooking baked goods, as baking parchment will fly up. These inexpensive mats can be bought from budget and homeware shops, and cut to size to fit your appliance.

1 ROAST VEGGIES

2 CRISP CHICKPEAS

3 CRUMBED FOODS

4 PIZZA & CALZONE

5 MEATBALLS & SAUSAGES

HEALTHIER SNACKS

Convenience and satisfaction are key when it comes to snacks. With the air fryer, you can create healthy, tempting snacks instead of reaching for junk food filled with empty calories or laden with sugar.

CAULIFLOWER FILO TRIANGLES

1 small onion (80g), cut into
   thin wedges
250g (8oz) cauliflower,
   finely chopped
2 garlic cloves, crushed
½ tsp ground turmeric
½ tsp ground ginger
¼ tsp ground cinnamon,
   plus extra, to dust
extra virgin olive oil cooking spray
75g (2½oz) feta, crumbled
2 tbsp roasted chopped almonds
2 tbsp coarsely chopped coriander
   (cilantro)
2 tbsp coarsely chopped
   flat-leaf parsley
12 sheets of filo pastry
to serve: lemon wedges and
   coriander (cilantro) leaves

1 Preheat a 5.3-litre air fryer to 180°C/350°F for 3 minutes.

2 Combine onion, cauliflower and garlic in a medium bowl, then sprinkle with combined spices; spray generously with oil.

3 Taking care, line the air-fryer basket with baking parchment. Put the cauliflower mixture in the basket; at 180°C/350°F, cook for 5 minutes until cauliflower is tender.

4 Transfer cooked cauliflower mixture to a bowl. Add feta, almonds and herbs to the bowl; stir to combine. Allow to cool. (Alternatively, spread out mixture on a tray and place in the freezer to chill for 5 minutes.)

5 Stack 2 sheets of pastry together, spraying between layers with oil. Cut stacked pastry lengthways into three strips. Place a heaped tablespoon of cauliflower mixture in the corner of one pastry strip, leaving a 1cm (½in) border. Fold opposite corner of pastry diagonally across filling to form a triangle; continue folding to the end of the pastry strip, retaining the triangular shape. Place, seam-side down, on a tray. Repeat with remaining pastry sheets, cooking spray and cauliflower mixture to make a total of 18 filo triangles. Spray triangles with oil; dust with extra cinnamon.

6 Place half of the filo triangles in the basket; at 180°C/350°F, cook for 10 minutes. Turn triangles over; cook for a further 10 minutes until golden. Transfer to a wire rack. Repeat cooking with remaining filo triangles.

7 Serve filo triangles with lemon wedges and coriander leaves.

prep + cook time 1 hour (+ cooling)
makes 18

GREEN FALAFEL
& TAHINI SAUCE

2½ cups (375g) frozen edamame
400g (12½oz) can chickpeas,
    drained, rinsed
1 medium onion (150g), chopped
3 garlic cloves
1 cup (30g) coarsely chopped
    flat-leaf parsley
½ cup (25g) coarsely chopped mint
1 cup (50g) coarsely chopped
    coriander (cilantro)
½ cup (75g) plain
    (all-purpose) flour
1 tsp fine salt
2 tsp ground cumin
1 tsp Moroccan spice mix
extra virgin olive oil cooking spray
to serve: chargrilled pitta breads,
    extra herbs and lemon wedges

TAHINI SAUCE
½ cup (140g) Greek-style yogurt
1½ tbsp tahini
1 garlic clove, crushed
2 tsp lemon juice

1 Place frozen edamame in a bowl; pour over boiling water. Allow to stand for 1 minute; drain. Cool under cold running water. Process 2 cups (300g) of the edamame, the chickpeas, onion, garlic, herbs, flour, salt, cumin and spice mix until finely chopped. Shape heaped tablespoons of mixture into approximately 26 oval falafel; place on a tray lined with cling film. Refrigerate for 1 hour to firm.
2 Meanwhile, to make tahini sauce, whisk ingredients in a small bowl until smooth; season to taste.
3 Preheat a 5.3-litre air fryer to 180°C/350°F for 3 minutes.

4 Spray falafel generously with oil. Taking care, place half of the falafel in the air-fryer basket; at 180°C/350°F, cook for 12 minutes, turning halfway through cooking time, or until golden. Transfer to a tray; cover to keep warm. Repeat cooking with the remaining falafel.
5 Fill chargrilled pitta breads with falafel, remaining edamame and extra herbs; drizzle with tahini sauce. Serve with lemon wedges.

TIP Sprinkle the tahini sauce with Moroccan spice mix, if you like.

**prep + cook time
40 minutes
(+ refrigeration)
serves 4**

SUN-DRIED TOMATO & FETA POLENTA CHIPS

3 cups (750ml) chicken or
   vegetable stock
1 cup (170g) instant polenta
30g (1oz) butter, chopped
½ cup (40g) finely grated Parmesan
90g (3oz) sun-dried tomatoes,
   no added oil, finely chopped
⅓ cup (20g) chopped basil leaves
100g (3oz) feta, crumbled
olive oil cooking spray
to serve: sea salt flakes

SALSA VERDE
2 tbsp red wine vinegar
2 tbsp capers, coarsely chopped
1 shallot, finely chopped
½ cup (25g) basil leaves,
   coarsely chopped
1 cup (20g) flat-leaf parsley leaves,
   coarsely chopped
½ cup (125ml) extra virgin olive oil

1 Bring stock to the boil in a large, deep saucepan; add polenta in a thin, steady stream, whisking until the mixture comes to the boil. Reduce heat to low, cook, stirring with a long-handled wooden spoon or whisk, for 10 minutes until mixture is soft and thick. Stir in butter, Parmesan, sun-dried tomatoes and basil.
2 Grease a deep 20cm (8in) square cake tin; line bottom and sides with baking parchment. Spread half of the polenta mixture over the bottom of the tin; scatter with half of the feta. Spread remaining polenta over feta; scatter with remaining feta, pressing it gently into the polenta. Cover tin. Refrigerate for 3 hours to firm.

3 Preheat a 7-litre air fryer to 200°C/400°F for 3 minutes.
4 Turn out polenta onto a chopping board and cut into 18 chips; spray generously all over with oil.
5 Spray the air-fryer basket with oil. Taking care, place polenta chips in the basket; at 200°C/400°F, cook for 15 minutes, turning halfway through cooking time, or until golden brown and crisp.
6 Meanwhile, to make salsa verde, combine ingredients in a bowl.
7 Sprinkle polenta chips with sea salt flakes and serve with salsa verde.

**prep + cook time
50 minutes
(+ refrigeration)
makes 18**

TIP Smooth ricotta is available in tubs in the refrigerated section of the supermarket.

HERB BAKED RICOTTA
WITH VEGGIE DIPPERS

---

2 x 60g (2oz) round flatbreads
20g (¾oz) butter, melted
½ tsp Italian-style dried herb mix
500g (1lb) thick smooth ricotta
   (see tip)
1 egg, lightly beaten
⅓ cup (25g) finely grated Parmesan
1 tbsp thyme leaves
¼ tsp dried chilli flakes
to serve: extra thyme leaves,
   extra virgin olive oil, baby rainbow
   carrots, baby cucumbers, radishes
   and Little Gem lettuce

1 Preheat a 7-litre air fryer to 180°C/350°F for 3 minutes.
2 Brush flatbread rounds with butter and sprinkle herb mix over the top.
3 Taking care, place one of the flatbread rounds in the air-fryer basket, then place a wire rack on top; at 180°C/350°F, cook for 3 minutes or until golden and crisp. Transfer to a plate to cool. Repeat cooking with remaining flatbread round. Once cooled, cut flatbread rounds into wedges.
4 Meanwhile, place ricotta, egg, Parmesan, thyme and chilli in a medium bowl, then season with salt and pepper; stir to combine. Divide mixture between two 300ml ovenproof baking dishes.
5 Place dishes in the air-fryer basket; at 180°C/350°F, cook for 20 minutes until ricotta is golden and set. Remove dishes from the air fryer.
6 Sprinkle baked ricottas with extra thyme leaves and drizzle with olive oil. Serve warm with flatbread wedges, baby carrots, baby cucumbers, radishes, and lettuce.

**prep + cook time
40 minutes serves 6**

TIP You can find spring roll wrappers in the freezer section of Asian grocers and supermarkets. Allow to thaw before using.

VEGETABLE SPRING ROLLS

50g (1½oz) dried vermicelli
  rice noodles
1 garlic clove, crushed
2 tbsp finely chopped fresh
  root ginger
1 shallot, thinly sliced
1 large carrot (180g), cut into
  matchsticks
2 cups (160g) shredded Chinese leaf
  (napa cabbage)
½ tsp Chinese five-spice powder
1 tsp sesame oil
2 tsp groundnut oil
2 tbsp tamari
1 tsp cornflour (cornstarch)
10 x 21.5cm (8¾in) frozen spring roll
  wrappers, thawed (see tip)
cooking oil spray
to serve: coriander (cilantro)
  and lime wedges

1 Place vermicelli in a medium bowl of boiling water for 2 minutes until soft; drain well. Using scissors, snip noodles into shorter lengths.
2 Line the basket of a 5.3-litre air fryer with baking parchment, then place garlic, ginger, shallot, carrot, Chinese leaf, five-spice powder, and sesame and groundnut oils in the basket; toss to combine. Set temperature to 180°C/350°F; cook for 5 minutes until vegetables are soft.
3 Taking care, transfer vegetable mixture to a bowl. Combine tamari and cornflour in a separate, small bowl. Add cornflour mixture to vegetable mixture with vermicelli; toss to combine. Allow to cool to room temperature.

4 Place a spring roll wrapper on a flat work surface. Place ¼ cup of the filling in a line one-third up from the bottom edge, leaving a 1.5cm (¾in) border on each side. Fold over once, then fold in the sides and roll up to enclose filling; brush the join with a little water to seal. Repeat with remaining spring roll wrappers and filling.
5 Preheat the air fryer to 180°C/350°F for 3 minutes.
6 Spray spring rolls generously with oil. Taking care, place half of the spring rolls in the air-fryer basket; at 180°C/350°F, cook for 12 minutes until golden brown. Transfer to a wire rack. Repeat cooking with remaining spring rolls.
7 Serve spring rolls with coriander and lime wedges.

SERVE IT Try the spring rolls with the Chilli Peanut Dressing on page 75.

**prep + cook time
45 minutes makes 10**

23

PICKLE CHIPS
WITH RANCH DIPPING SAUCE

⅓ cup (75g) plain (all-purpose) flour
⅔ cup (160ml) buttermilk
1 tbsp hot chilli sauce
2¼ cups (170g) panko breadcrumbs
700g (1½lb) jar sliced bread and
    butter pickles, drained
olive oil cooking spray
to serve: sea salt flakes

RANCH DIPPING SAUCE
½ cup (150g) whole-egg mayonnaise
½ cup (120g) light soured cream
2 tbsp chopped dill
2 tbsp chopped chives
1 small garlic clove, crushed
1 tbsp lemon juice

1 Place flour in a shallow bowl. Lightly beat buttermilk and chilli sauce in a second shallow bowl and place breadcrumbs in a third shallow bowl. Dust pickles in flour, shaking off excess, dip in buttermilk mixture, then coat in breadcrumbs; spray generously all over with oil.
2 Preheat a 7-litre air fryer to 200°C/400°F for 3 minutes.
3 Taking care, place one-third of the pickles in the air-fryer basket in a single layer; at 200°C/400°F; cook for 6 minutes until golden. Transfer to a plate. Repeat cooking with remaining pickles.
4 Meanwhile, to make ranch dipping sauce, combine ingredients in a small bowl.
5 Sprinkle pickle chips with sea salt flakes and serve with ranch dipping sauce.

**prep + cook time
40 minutes
serves 6**

FRIES TO FIGHT FOR

GREEK FETA & OREGANO FRIES

prep + cook time 15 minutes serves 4

Preheat a 5.3-litre air fryer to 200°C/400°F for 3 minutes. Place 700g (1½lb) frozen French fries in the air-fryer basket with 8 unpeeled garlic cloves, then spray with cooking oil; at 200°C/400°F, cook for 10 minutes, turning halfway through cooking time, or until fries are golden. Tip fries into a large bowl. Crumble over 100g (3oz) feta and sprinkle with 1 tsp sea salt flakes and 1 tsp dried oregano; toss to combine.

COURGETTE FRIES

prep + cook time 30 minutes serves 4

Cut 3 large courgettes (zucchini) (450g) in half crossways. Cut courgette halves into "fries" 1cm (½in) thick. Combine ⅔ cup (70g) ground almonds (or panko breadcrumbs), ½ cup (50g) finely grated Parmesan, 1 tsp each of smoked paprika and finely chopped rosemary or oregano, and a pinch of ground chilli in a bowl. Preheat a 5.3-litre air fryer to 200°C/400°F for 3 minutes. Toss courgette fries with 2 tbsp extra virgin olive oil, then coat in almond mixture. Place half of the fries in the air-fryer basket in a single layer; at 200°C/400°F, cook for 10 minutes, turning halfway through cooking time, until fries are golden. Transfer to a plate; cover to keep warm. Repeat with remaining fries. Season to taste. Serve with Greek Yogurt Dipping Sauce (see recipe right).

HALLOUMI FRIES

prep + cook time 15 minutes serves 4

Cut 2 x 225g (7oz) blocks of Halloumi horizontally into three slices each. Cut each slice into three "fries"; you will have 18 in total. Combine ½ cup (75g) plain (all-purpose) flour, 1 tsp each of ground cumin and ground coriander, and ½ tsp smoked paprika in a bowl. Preheat a 5.3-litre air fryer to 200°C/400°F for 3 minutes. Spray the air-fryer basket with cooking oil. Spray Halloumi fries with cooking oil, then coat in flour mixture. Place the Halloumi fries in the basket in a single layer; at 200°C/400°F, cook for 5 minutes until fries are golden. Serve with Greek Yogurt Dipping Sauce (see recipe below).

GREEK YOGURT DIPPING SAUCE

prep time 5 minutes makes 1¼ cups

Combine 1¼ cups (350g) Greek-style yogurt, 1 tsp finely grated lemon zest, 1 smashed garlic clove, 2 tbsp finely chopped dill and 2 tbsp finely chopped mint; season with salt and pepper to taste. Remove the garlic clove when ready to serve.

TIP Use just one herb in the recipe, if you like.

GREEK FETA & OREGANO FRIES

HALLOUMI FRIES

COURGETTE FRIES

GREEK YOGURT DIPPING SAUCE

COURGETTE BALLS
WITH LEMON YOGURT

700g (1½lb) courgettes (zucchini),
   coarsely grated
2 tsp coarse cooking salt
1 egg, lightly beaten
½ cup (120g) fresh firm ricotta,
   crumbled
⅓ cup (25g) finely grated Parmesan
1 cup (100g) packaged breadcrumbs
½ cup (15g) finely chopped
   flat-leaf parsley
3 spring onions (scallions),
   thinly sliced
olive oil cooking spray
¾ cup (200g) Greek-style yogurt
1 small garlic clove, crushed
2 tsp finely grated lemon zest
1 tbsp lemon juice
to serve: sea salt flakes

1 Place courgettes in a colander and sprinkle with salt; allow to stand for 20 minutes. Using your hands, squeeze courgettes very firmly to remove any excess liquid; transfer to a large bowl.
2 Add egg, ricotta, Parmesan, breadcrumbs, parsley and spring onions to bowl, then season with salt and pepper; stir until well combined. With damp hands, shape heaped tablespoons of courgette mixture into balls; place on a tray lined with baking parchment. Spray all over with oil.
3 Preheat a 7-litre air fryer to 180°C/350°F for 3 minutes. Cut out a 22cm (9in) round from a piece of baking parchment.
4 Taking care, line the air-fryer basket with the baking parchment round. Place courgette balls in the basket; at 180°C/350°F, cook for 25 minutes, turning after 15 minutes of cooking time, until golden and cooked through.
5 Meanwhile, to make lemon yogurt, combine remaining ingredients in a small bowl.
6 Sprinkle courgette balls with sea salt flakes and serve with lemon yogurt.

**prep + cook time
45 minutes (+ standing)
makes 24**

29

CRISPY PEPPERONI-FLAVOURED PEAS & BEANS

2 x 400g (12½oz) cans chickpeas, drained, rinsed
200g (6½oz) frozen edamame, thawed
⅓ cup (80ml) extra virgin olive oil
2 tsp garlic granules (see tip)
2 tsp fennel seeds
2 tsp dried chilli flakes
2 tsp onion powder
2 tsp smoked paprika
1 tsp sea salt flakes
¼ cup (50g) pumpkin seeds (pepitas) (optional)

1 Preheat a 5.3-litre air fryer to 180°C/350°F for 3 minutes.
2 Place chickpeas on a tray lined with kitchen paper; pat with more kitchen paper until well dried. Repeat with edamame on fresh kitchen paper.
3 Toss chickpeas with 2 tablespoons of the oil in a large bowl. Combine garlic granules, fennel seeds, chilli flakes, onion powder, paprika and salt flakes in a small bowl. Sprinkle half of the spice mix over chickpeas.
4 Taking care, place the chickpeas in the air-fryer basket; at 180°C/350°F, cook for 15 minutes, turning twice during cooking time, or until crisp and golden. Add the pumpkin seeds, if you like, 2 minutes before the end of cooking time. Transfer to a clean bowl to cool.
5 Combine edamame, remaining oil and remaining spice mix in a bowl. Place edamame in the air-fryer basket; at 180°C/350°F, cook for 12 minutes, turning twice during cooking time, or until crisp and darkened. Transfer edamame to bowl with chickpeas to cool.

KEEP IT Crisp peas and beans mixture will keep in an airtight container for up to 1 week.

**prep + cook time
40 minutes
makes 3 cups**

TIP Garlic granules, sometimes sold as granulated garlic, are sold in small packets or jars alongside other spices in the supermarket.

BACON & LEEK FRITTATAS

1 tbsp extra virgin olive oil
3 centre-cut (back) bacon rashers
  (105g), finely chopped
½ small leek (100g), thinly sliced
2 eggs
⅓ cup (80ml) single (light) cream
2 tbsp grated mozzarella
1 tbsp grated Cheddar
1 tbsp grated Parmesan
to serve: sea salt flakes (optional)

1 Grease a 12-hole
(1 tablespoon/20ml)
mini muffin tin.
2 Heat oil in a medium
frying pan; cook bacon,
stirring, for 3 minutes
or until browned lightly.
Add leek; cook, stirring,
for 5 minutes or until leek
softens and bacon is crisp.
Allow to cool for 2 minutes.
3 Preheat a 7-litre
air fryer to 180°C/350°F
for 3 minutes.
4 Spoon bacon mixture into
muffin tin holes. Lightly
whisk eggs and cream in a
jug, then season with salt
and pepper. Combine the
three cheeses in a small
bowl; stir 2 tablespoons
of the cheese into egg
mixture. Pour mixture into
muffin tin holes; sprinkle
with remaining cheese.

5 Taking care, gently lower
muffin tin into the air-fryer
basket; at 180°C/350°F,
cook for 5 minutes. Cover
tin with greased foil; cook
for a further 5 minutes
until frittatas are golden
and cooked through.
Remove muffin tin from
the air fryer. Leave frittatas
in tin for 5 minutes before
turning, top-side up, onto
a wire rack to cool.
6 Sprinkle frittatas with
sea salt flakes to serve,
if you like.

prep + cook time
30 minutes
makes 12

SRIRACHA VEGETABLE TEMPURA

1 bunch of asparagus (175g)
1 head of broccoli (400g)
1 medium carrot (120g)
150g (4½oz) oyster mushrooms
⅔ cup (100g) self-raising flour
½ tsp fine salt
1 egg
1 tbsp sriracha chilli sauce
¾ cup (180ml) chilled
    sparkling water
2¼ cups (185g) panko breadcrumbs
100ml extra virgin olive oil
to serve: tamari or ponzu sauce,
    finely chopped red chilli and
    toasted sesame seeds

1 Trim asparagus. Cut broccoli into florets. Cut carrot into 5mm (¼in) slices on a diagonal. Separate mushrooms, if needed.

2 Combine flour and salt in a large bowl. Place egg, sriracha and sparkling water in a jug; whisk to combine. Add egg mixture to flour mixture; whisk until just combined.

3 Preheat a 5.3-litre air fryer to 180°C/350°F for 3 minutes. Line a tray with baking parchment and top a second tray with a wire rack.

4 Place breadcrumbs in a bowl; drizzle over oil. Using your fingertips, rub the oil into the crumbs until well combined. Working with one vegetable piece at a time, dip in batter, allowing excess to drip off, then coat in breadcrumb mixture; place on lined tray. Continue coating until you have 6–8 vegetable pieces ready to cook.

5 Taking care, place the vegetables in the air-fryer basket in a single layer; at 180°C/350°F, cook for 5 minutes, turning halfway through cooking time, or until golden brown. Transfer to the wire rack over the second tray.

6 Repeat coating and cooking remaining vegetable pieces in four more batches.

7 Serve vegetable tempura with tamari sprinkled with finely chopped red chilli and toasted sesame seeds.

**prep + cook time
40 minutes
serves 4**

DRIED WATERMELON

DRIED PINEAPPLE

DRIED APPLE

DRIED KIWI FRUIT

DRIED PINEAPPLE

Lightly spray two of the included racks of an 11-litre air fryer with olive oil cooking spray. Cut a pineapple in half crossways through the middle (reserve the other half for another use). Peel, then remove the core with an apple corer. Thinly slice pineapple into 2mm-thick rings. Arrange rings over racks in a single layer. Taking care, place racks in the air fryer. Set air fryer to dehydration setting and set temperature to 70°C/160°F; cook for 4 hours, rotating racks halfway through cooking time, or until pineapple is dried. Remove racks from the air fryer. Leave pineapple on racks to cool. Store in an airtight container in a cool, dry place for up to 2 weeks.

DRIED APPLE

Lightly spray two of the included racks of an 11-litre air fryer with olive oil cooking spray. Using a mandolin or V-slicer, thinly slice 2 red apples into slices 1–2mm thick. Arrange apple slices over racks in a single layer. Taking care, place racks in the air fryer. Set air fryer to dehydration setting and set temperature to 70°C/160°F; cook for 4 hours, rotating racks halfway through cooking time, or until apple is dried and crisp. Remove racks from the air fryer. Leave apple on racks to cool. Store in an airtight container in a cool, dry place for up to 2 weeks.

DEHYDRATED SNACKS

DRIED WATERMELON

Lightly spray two of the included racks of an 11-litre air fryer with olive oil cooking spray. Using a sharp knife, cut an 800g (1½lb) wedge of watermelon into slices 2–3mm thick. Arrange watermelon slices over racks in a single layer. Taking care, place racks in the air fryer. Set air fryer to dehydration setting and set temperature to 70°C/160°F; cook for 4 hours, rotating racks halfway through cooking time, or until watermelon is dried. Remove racks from the air fryer. Leave watermelon on racks to cool. Store in an airtight container in a cool, dry place for up to 2 weeks.

DRIED KIWI FRUIT

Lightly spray two of the included racks of an 11-litre air fryer with olive oil cooking spray. Peel 4 kiwi fruit, then thinly slice into 2mm-thick slices. Arrange kiwi fruit slices over racks in a single layer. Taking care, place racks in the air fryer. Set air fryer to dehydration setting and set temperature to 70°C/160°F; cook for 4 hours, rotating racks halfway through cooking time, or until kiwi fruit is dried. Remove racks from the air fryer. Leave kiwi fruit on racks to cool. Store in an airtight container in a cool, dry place for up to 2 weeks.

prep + cook time
4 hours 15 minutes
(+ cooling)

4 WAYS

SPINACH & FETA TWISTS

250g (8oz) frozen spinach, thawed
2 sheets of frozen puff pastry,
    just thawed
100g (3oz) feta, crumbled
½ cup (40g) finely grated Parmesan
cooking oil spray

1 Place spinach in a fine sieve; squeeze out excess liquid. Coarsely chop spinach, then pat dry between sheets of kitchen paper.
2 Place a pastry sheet on a tray lined with baking parchment. Top with half of the spinach, half of the combined cheeses, then the remaining sheet of pastry; scatter over remaining spinach and cheeses. Cut pastry stack in half; place one half on top of the other half and press down firmly. Place pastry stack in the freezer for 5 minutes to firm, then cut crossways into 24 strips. Pinch one end of a strip, then twist from that end to the other end until 20cm (8in) long; pinch other end to seal. Repeat twisting with remaining strips.
3 Preheat a 5.3-litre air fryer to 200°C/400°F for 3 minutes.
4 Spray the air-fryer basket with oil. Taking care, place half of the twists in the basket; at 200°C/400°F, cook for 5 minutes until golden brown and cooked through. Transfer to a wire rack to cool. Repeat cooking with remaining twists.

KEEP IT Twists will keep in an airtight container for up to 3 days.

**prep + cook time
30 minutes
makes 24**

VEGGIE CHIPS

3 large orange carrots (540g)
3 medium purple carrots (360g)
3 medium parsnips (750g)
1 medium beetroot (175g)
extra virgin olive oil cooking spray
to serve: sea salt flakes

SWAP IT
Get crisping with other veggies: try sweet potato and Jerusalem artichokes. Jerusalem artichokes pop up around winter and look rather unimpressive, but don't let that put you off, as they taste amazing.

1 Preheat a 5.3-litre air fryer to 120°C/250°F for 3 minutes.
2 Cut carrots, parsnips and beetroot in half lengthways. Using a mandolin or V-slicer, slice vegetables, cut-side down, into 2mm-thick slices.
3 Taking care, place purple carrot and beetroot slices in the air-fryer basket; at 120°C/250°F, cook for 30 minutes, stirring halfway through cooking time and separating the slices, or until crisp. Transfer purple carrot chips to a tray; cover to keep warm. Cook beetroot chips for a further 5 minutes; transfer to tray with purple carrot chips. Spray chips with oil and sprinkle with sea salt flakes. Allow to cool.
4 Repeat cooking with parsnip slices, then orange carrot slices, cooking at 120°C/250°F for 25 minutes each. Add to tray with purple carrot and beetroot chips; spray with oil and sprinkle with more sea salt flakes or one of the seasoning variations below.

SEASONING VARIATIONS
fennel & chilli Using a mortar and pestle, crush 2 teaspoons fennel seeds until coarsely ground; stir in 1 teaspoon dried chilli flakes until evenly mixed.
sumac & thyme Combine 1 teaspoon sumac and 2 teaspoons chopped thyme.
smoked paprika Combine 1 teaspoon smoked paprika and 1 teaspoon onion powder.

KEEP IT Veggie chips will keep in an airtight container for up to 4 days.

prep + cook time 1¾ hours
serves 6

PEAR & RICOTTA FRITTERS

¼ cup (60ml) buttermilk
1 egg
125g (4oz) smooth ricotta
2 tbsp caster (superfine) sugar
½ tsp ground cinnamon
¾ cup (105g) self-raising flour
1 large, firm pear such as Corella or
   Packham (200g), peeled, grated
olive oil cooking spray
1 cup (280g) vanilla yogurt
2 tbsp honey

1 Preheat a 7-litre air fryer to 200°C/400°F for 3 minutes.
2 Whisk the buttermilk, egg, ricotta, sugar and cinnamon in a medium bowl until well combined. Sift flour over ricotta mixture; mix to combine. Fold in pear.
3 Taking care, line the air-fryer basket with baking parchment. Drop 6 heaped tablespoons of fritter mixture onto the parchment about 2cm (¾in) apart. Using the back of a spoon, smooth the surface of the fritters to flatten slightly, then spray with oil; at 200°C/400°F, cook for 8 minutes, turning halfway through cooking time, until golden and cooked through. Transfer to a plate; cover loosely with foil to keep warm. Repeat cooking with remaining fritter mixture and oil spray to make 12 fritters in total.
4 Serve fritters warm, dolloped with yogurt and drizzled with honey.

**prep + cook time
30 minutes
makes 12**

FAVOURITE DINNERS

When you have a family to feed or are ravenous after arriving home from work, getting a meal on the table fast is the priority. The air fryer, with its fast heating and rapid air circulation, makes this possible.

BACON 'N' CHEESE BURGERS

500g (1lb) beef mince (ground beef)
1 egg
¾ cup (75g) panko breadcrumbs
2 tbsp barbecue sauce
1 tsp smoked paprika
1 garlic clove, crushed
¼ cup (70g) low-sugar
   tomato ketchup
olive oil cooking spray
4 slices of Cheddar
4 back bacon rashers (140g)
4 large brioche buns (400g)
2 tbsp whole-egg mayonnaise
4 Little Gem lettuce leaves
⅓ cup (40g) burger pickles
to serve: sweet potato fries

1 Using your hands, combine beef, egg, breadcrumbs, barbecue sauce, paprika, garlic and 1 tablespoon of the tomato ketchup in a large bowl, then season with salt and pepper; mix well. Shape mixture into four patties the same size as the brioche buns; ensure they will all fit in the air-fryer basket. Spray all over with oil.

2 Preheat a 7-litre air fryer to 180°C/350°F for 3 minutes.

3 Spray the air-fryer basket with oil. Taking care, arrange patties in the basket; at 180°C/350°F, cook for 10 minutes, turning halfway through cooking time, or until browned and cooked through. Transfer to a plate and top each with a slice of Cheddar; cover loosely with foil to keep warm.

4 Taking care, arrange bacon in the air-fryer basket. Reset the temperature to 200°C/400°F; cook for 5 minutes until crisp.

5 Split and toast brioche buns. Spread bun bases with mayonnaise, then top with lettuce, patties, bacon, pickles and remaining tomato ketchup; sandwich together with bun tops.

6 Serve burgers with sweet potato fries.

prep + cook time
30 minutes
serves 4

SWEET POTATO PARMIGIANA

4 small orange sweet potatoes
  (1kg), scrubbed
2 tbsp extra virgin olive oil
⅓ cup (85g) tomato pasta sauce
125g (4oz) shaved leg ham
⅔ cup (70g) coarsely grated
  mozzarella
2 tbsp finely grated Parmesan
to serve: extra finely grated
  Parmesan and basil leaves

1 Pierce sweet potatoes all over with a small, sharp knife or fork; rub with oil and season with salt and pepper. Wrap each sweet potato individually in foil.
2 Preheat a 7-litre air fryer to 200°C/400°F for 3 minutes.
3 Taking care, place sweet potatoes in the air-fryer basket in a single layer; at 200°C/400°F, cook for 50 minutes, turning halfway through cooking time, or until tender. Transfer to a plate; remove and discard foil.
4 Cut sweet potatoes in half lengthways, being careful not to cut all the way through; open out so that the flesh sides are facing up. Spoon over pasta sauce, then top with ham and cheeses.
5 Taking care, place topped sweet potatoes in the air-fryer basket in a single layer; at 200°C/400°F, cook for 5 minutes or until cheese topping is golden and melted.
6 Serve each sweet potato parmigiana topped with extra finely grated Parmesan and basil leaves.

MATCH IT Italian-style Rice Salad, page 98.

**prep + cook time
1 hour 10 minutes
serves 4**

BEEF SKEWERS
WITH GARLIC TZATZIKI

You will need 8 x 22cm (8¾in)
metal skewers for this recipe.
1 tbsp finely grated lemon zest
2 tbsp lemon juice
1 tsp dried oregano
1 tbsp extra virgin olive oil
3 garlic cloves, crushed
500g (1lb) beef rump steak or
sirloin, cut into 2.5cm (1in) pieces
1 medium red pepper (200g),
deseeded and cut into 3cm
(1¼in) pieces
1 medium yellow pepper (200g),
deseeded and cut into 3cm
(1¼in) pieces
220g (7oz) tub tzatziki (see tips)
to serve: salad leaves and
lemon cheeks

1 Combine lemon zest and juice, oregano, oil and two-thirds of the garlic in a shallow dish; add beef and toss to coat. Thread beef and both peppers, alternately, onto skewers.
2 Preheat a 7-litre air fryer to 200°C/400°F for 3 minutes.
3 Taking care, place skewers in the air-fryer basket; at 200°C/400°F, cook for 8 minutes, turning halfway through cooking time, for medium or until cooked to your liking.
4 Meanwhile, stir remaining garlic into tzatziki in the tub; transfer to a serving bowl.

5 Place skewers on a platter. Serve with tzatziki, salad leaves and lemon cheeks.

TIPS If you are using a smaller air fryer, you will need to cook the skewers in batches. For homemade tzatziki, coarsely grate ½ small Lebanese cucumber and squeeze out the excess liquid; combine in a bowl with ¾ cup (210g) Greek-style yogurt and ½ crushed garlic clove, then season with salt and pepper.

prep + cook time
30 minutes serves 4

MATCH IT Greek-style Potatoes, page 145.

JAMAICAN FISH TACOS

1 tsp ground allspice
½ tsp dried thyme
1½ tsp cayenne pepper
1 tsp ground cinnamon
1½ tbsp garlic powder
2 tbsp light soft brown sugar
¼ cup (60ml) olive oil
800g (1½lb) firm white skinless fish
    fillets, cut into long pieces (see tip)
16 x 14cm (5½in) flour tortillas
cooking oil spray
to serve: lime cheeks

AVOCADO CREAM
2 medium avocados (500g)
½ cup (120g) soured cream
2 tbsp lime juice

SLAW
350g (11oz) green cabbage,
    shredded
2 cups (60g) coriander
    (cilantro) leaves
1 small red onion (100g),
    thinly sliced
1 long green chilli,
    deseeded, thinly sliced

1 Combine allspice, thyme, cayenne pepper, cinnamon, garlic powder, brown sugar and oil in a medium bowl; add fish and toss to coat. Season with salt.
2 To make avocado cream, blend or process ingredients until smooth; season to taste.
3 Wrap tortillas in foil. Place in the basket of a 5.3-litre air fryer; at 180°C/350°F, cook for 5 minutes to preheat the air fryer and warm through the tortillas.
4 Taking care, transfer tortillas to a plate; cover to keep warm. Spray fish with oil and place in the air-fryer basket; at 180°C/350°F, cook for 8 minutes, turning halfway through cooking time, or until cooked through.

5 Meanwhile, to make slaw, combine ingredients in a bowl.
6 Fill warm tortillas with fish and slaw; top with avocado cream. Serve with lime cheeks.

TIP Cut fish fillets lengthways on the diagonal into 1.5cm (¾in) wide, 12cm (4¾in) long strips.

PREP IT Fish can be prepared to the end of step 1 up to 4 hours ahead. Avocado cream and slaw can also be prepared up to 4 hours ahead. Refrigerate until needed.

prep + cook time
25 minutes serves 8

SWAP IT Replace all the spices with a sachet of taco seasoning.

COCONUT HONEY PRAWNS

½ cup (75g) plain (all-purpose) flour
2 eggs
1½ cups (115g) unsweetened
    shredded coconut
1 cup (75g) panko breadcrumbs
600g (1¼lb) peeled uncooked
    prawns (shrimp), tails intact
olive oil cooking spray
to serve: steamed jasmine rice
    and steamed pak choi (bok choy)

HONEY SAUCE
⅓ cup (120g) honey
1 tbsp lemon juice
1 tbsp soy sauce
1 tsp finely grated fresh root ginger
1 garlic clove, crushed
½ tsp Chinese five-spice powder
2 tsp cornflour (cornstarch)

1 Place flour in a shallow bowl. Lightly whisk eggs in a second shallow bowl. Combine coconut and breadcrumbs in a third shallow bowl. Dust prawns in flour, shaking off excess, dip in egg, then coat in coconut mixture; place on a tray. Refrigerate for 30 minutes.

2 Meanwhile, to make honey sauce, combine honey, lemon juice, soy sauce, ginger, garlic, and five-spice powder in a small saucepan over a medium heat; cook, stirring, for 2 minutes or until honey melts. Bring to the boil. Blend cornflour and 1 tablespoon water in a small cup. Whisk cornflour mixture into sauce; cook, stirring, for 2 minutes or until slightly thickened. Remove from heat; cover to keep warm.

3 Preheat a 7-litre air fryer to 200°C/400°F for 3 minutes.

4 Spray prawns generously all over with oil. Taking care, place half of the prawns in the air-fryer basket in a single layer; at 200°C/400°F, cook for 6 minutes, turning halfway through cooking time, until golden and just cooked through. Transfer to a plate; cover loosely with foil to keep warm. Repeat cooking with remaining prawns.

5 Serve prawns with steamed rice and steamed pak choi, drizzled with honey sauce.

**prep + cook time
40 minutes
(+ refrigeration)
serves 4**

HERBY LAMB KOFTAS
WITH GREEN TAHINI

500g (1lb) lamb mince (ground lamb)
2 tsp ground cumin
2 tsp ground coriander
1 tsp paprika
1 egg, lightly beaten
¼ cup (25g) packaged breadcrumbs
½ cup (25g) finely chopped mint
½ cup (15g) finely chopped
   flat-leaf parsley
olive oil cooking spray
½ cup (140g) Greek-style yogurt
2 tbsp tahini
2 tbsp lemon juice
to serve: grilled pitta bread rounds,
   cut into wedges

TOMATO SALAD
250g (8oz) mixed baby
   tomatoes, halved
1 Lebanese cucumber,
   thickly sliced
2 tbsp mint leaves
2 tbsp flat-leaf parsley leaves
extra virgin olive oil, to drizzle

1 Using your hands, combine lamb, cumin, coriander, paprika, egg, breadcrumbs and half of each of the chopped mint and parsley in a bowl; mix well. With damp hands, shape level tablespoons of mince mixture into balls to make koftas; place on a tray. Spray all over with oil.
2 Preheat a 7-litre air fryer to 180°C/350°F for 3 minutes.
3 Spray the air-fryer basket with oil. Taking care, place koftas in the basket in a single layer; at 180°C/350°F, cook for 8 minutes, shaking the basket halfway through cooking time, until browned and cooked through.

4 Meanwhile, to make green tahini, combine yogurt, tahini, lemon juice and remaining chopped mint and parsley in a small bowl.
5 To make tomato salad, combine tomatoes, cucumber, mint and parsley on a platter; drizzle with oil and season with salt and pepper to taste.
6 Add koftas and green tahini to platter. Serve with grilled pitta bread.

MATCH IT Lentil Tabbouleh, page 98.

prep + cook time 35 minutes serves 4

BARBECUE BOURBON CHICKEN WINGS

½ cup (140g) barbecue sauce
¼ cup (60ml) bourbon
1 tbsp Dijon mustard
1.5kg (3lb) chicken wings
to serve: extra barbecue sauce

1 Combine barbecue sauce, bourbon and mustard in a large bowl; add chicken and toss to coat.
2 Preheat a 7-litre air fryer to 180°C/350°F for 3 minutes.
3 Taking care, place chicken in the air-fryer basket; at 180°C/350°F, cook for 20 minutes, basting and turning occasionally, or until cooked through.
4 Serve chicken brushed with extra barbecue sauce.

MATCH IT Feta, Dill & Bacon Potatoes, page 145.

**prep + cook time
30 minutes serves 4**

PICK-A-FLAVOUR PIZZA NIGHT

2 x 250g (8oz) fresh pizza dough
   balls (see tip)
⅔ cup (170g) tomato pasta sauce
1 medium red onion (170g),
   thinly sliced
4 back bacon rashers (140g), sliced
100g (3oz) pancetta, torn
1 cured chorizo (170g), sliced
300g (9½oz) mozzarella, sliced
1 small red chilli, sliced
to serve: basil leaves

1 Preheat a 5.3-litre air fryer to 180°C/350°F for 3 minutes.
2 Join dough balls into one large ball on a lightly floured work surface. Roll out into a 16cm x 26cm (6½in x 10½in) oval on a piece of baking parchment. Trim baking parchment so that it is 3cm (1¼in) larger all around than the dough base.
3 Spread pizza base with pasta sauce; top with onion, bacon, pancetta, chorizo, mozzarella and chilli (or choose another pizza flavour).
4 Taking care, and using the baking parchment as an aid, lower the pizza into the air-fryer basket. Reset the temperature to 170°C/340°F; cook for 15 minutes until pizza crust is golden and cooked through.
5 Serve pizza topped with basil leaves.

OTHER FLAVOURS
prawn Omit the meats and mozzarella, and replace with 8 uncooked peeled and deveined prawns (shrimp) tossed in 2 teaspoons extra virgin olive oil. Serve topped with rocket (arugula) and grated lemon zest.
gimme greens Omit the meats and replace with 175g (5½oz) halved broccolini (Tenderstem broccoli) stalks and ¼ cup (50g) halved kalamata olives. Serve topped with crumbled goat's cheese and grated lemon zest.
aubergine & ricotta Omit the meats and replace with 450g (14½oz) chargrilled aubergine (eggplant) slices and 100g (3oz) ricotta. Serve topped with pesto.

TIP You can find fresh dough balls in the refrigerated section of larger supermarkets.

prep + cook time
25 minutes serves 2

SALMON FISHCAKES
WITH LEMON & HERBS

3 medium floury potatoes (600g),
    coarsely chopped
2 tbsp olive oil
olive oil cooking spray
400g (12½oz) skinless boneless
    salmon fillets
2 spring onions (scallions),
    thinly sliced
2 tsp finely grated lemon zest
1 tbsp finely chopped dill or parsley
1 egg, lightly beaten
1½ cups (110g) panko breadcrumbs
Pick-a-Sauce (see pages 74–75)
to serve: lime wedges

1 Preheat a 5.3-litre air fryer to 180°C/350°F for 3 minutes.

2 Boil, steam or microwave potatoes until tender; drain. Mash potatoes with olive oil until smooth.

3 Meanwhile, spray the air-fryer basket with oil. Taking care, place salmon in the basket; at 180°C/350°F, cook for 6 minutes until salmon is cooked through. Pull out the air-fryer pan and basket; allow salmon to cool in the basket.

4 Flake salmon into the mashed potato; mash until salmon breaks into smaller pieces. Add spring onion, lemon zest, dill, egg and half of the breadcrumbs, then season with salt and pepper; stir to combine. With damp hands, shape mixture into eight patties; place on a tray. Freeze for 10 minutes to firm.

5 Coat patties in remaining breadcrumbs; spray generously with oil.

6 Place patties in the air-fryer basket; at 180°C/350°F, cook for 8 minutes, turning halfway through cooking time, or until golden and heated through.

7 Serve fishcakes with your choice of Pick-a-Sauce and lime wedges.

SWAP IT To make red curry fishcakes, use the equivalent weight of sweet potatoes instead of floury potatoes and stir 2 tablespoons Thai red curry paste into the mash; use coriander (cilantro) instead of dill.

**prep + cook time
45 minutes (+ cooling
& freezing)
makes 8**

TIP Short on time? Use a 475g (15oz) tub of mashed potato (or sweet potato) and 300g (9½oz) hot-smoked trout.

CHICKEN WINGS

4 WAYS

PINEAPPLE HULI-HULI

STICKY SESAME

STICKY POMEGRANATE

SMOKY BARBECUE

CHICKEN WINGS

prep + cook time 50 minutes (+ refrigeration) serves 4

Toss 1.5kg (3lb) chicken wings with chosen marinade below in a large bowl. Refrigerate for 1–2 hours. Preheat air fryer to 180°C/350°F for 3 minutes. Taking care, place chicken in the air-fryer basket; cook for 40 minutes, turning occasionally, until chicken is cooked.

STICKY SESAME

Combine 4 thinly sliced spring onions (scallions), 3 crushed garlic cloves, ¼ cup (60ml) each of soy sauce and Shaohsing rice wine, 3 tsp finely grated fresh root ginger and 2 tbsp light soft brown sugar in a bowl. Serve cooked wings topped with 2 tbsp toasted sesame seeds and extra sliced spring onion.

STICKY POMEGRANATE

Combine 1 cup (220g) firmly packed light soft brown sugar, 1½ cups (375ml) pomegranate juice, 3 tsp grated orange zest, 2 crushed garlic cloves, 1½ tbsp each of Worcestershire sauce and Dijon mustard, and ⅓ cup (80ml) tomato ketchup in a saucepan, stirring to mix through evenly. Bring to the boil; stir occasionally over a medium heat for 10 minutes or until reduced by half. Serve cooked wings topped with pomegranate seeds.

PINEAPPLE HULI-HULI

Combine ⅓ cup (110g) firmly packed light soft brown sugar, ⅔ cup (170ml) fresh pineapple juice, ½ cup (125ml) each of tomato ketchup and soy sauce, ⅓ cup (80ml) malt vinegar, 1 tbsp finely grated fresh root ginger and 2 crushed garlic cloves in a frying pan. Boil over a medium heat for 5 minutes. Sprinkle wings with 1 tbsp paprika before tossing in marinade. Serve cooked wings topped with coriander (cilantro).

SMOKY BARBECUE

Combine ½ cup (175g) honey, ½ cup (125ml) smoky barbecue sauce and 2 tbsp teriyaki sauce in a bowl. Serve cooked wings with thinly sliced long red chilli and lime wedges.

STUFFED AUBERGINE
WITH LENTILS

---

2 large aubergines (eggplants) (1kg),
  halved lengthways
2 tsp table salt
olive oil cooking spray
1 tbsp extra virgin olive oil
1 medium onion (150g),
  finely chopped
2 garlic cloves, crushed
1 tsp ground cumin
1 tsp smoked paprika
400g (12½oz) can brown lentils,
  drained, rinsed
400g (12½oz) can cherry tomatoes
¼ cup chopped oregano leaves
100g (3oz) feta, crumbled
⅓ cup (25g) finely grated Parmesan
to serve: extra oregano leaves

1 Using a small, sharp knife, score the cut side of aubergine halves in a diamond pattern without cutting all the way through; season with salt. Place, cut-side down, on a wire rack for 30 minutes; rinse and pat dry with kitchen paper. Using a teaspoon, carefully scoop out aubergine flesh, leaving a shell 1cm (½in) thick. Finely chop aubergine flesh. Spray aubergine shells with oil.

2 Preheat a 7-litre air fryer to 180°C/350°F for 3 minutes.

3 Taking care, place eggplant shells, cut-side up, in the air-fryer basket; at 180°C/350°F, cook for 12 minutes until softened.

4 Meanwhile, heat oil in a large frying pan over a medium-high heat; cook onion, stirring, for 5 minutes or until softened. Add garlic, cumin and paprika; cook, stirring, for 1 minute or until fragrant. Add aubergine flesh; cook, stirring occasionally, for 5 minutes or until tender. Add lentils and tomatoes; bring to a simmer. Stir in oregano; season with salt and pepper to taste. Allow to cool for 5 minutes. Stir half of the feta into the lentil mixture.

5 Transfer aubergine shells to a plate. Spoon lentil mixture into the shells, then sprinkle with Parmesan and remaining feta; spray lightly with oil.

6 Taking care, place stuffed aubergines in the air-fryer basket; at 180°C/350°F, cook for 8 minutes until lightly browned and tender.

7 Serve stuffed aubergines scattered with extra oregano leaves.

**prep + cook time
50 minutes (+ standing)
serves 4**

CHICKEN CHIMICHANGAS
WITH AVOCADO SALSA

3 cups (480g) shredded cooked chicken
30g (1oz) packet taco seasoning
1 cup (120g) coarsely grated Cheddar
200g (6½oz) jar taco sauce
4 x 20cm (8in) flour tortillas, slightly warmed
olive oil cooking spray
1 medium avocado (250g), diced
1 medium tomato (150g), chopped
½ small red onion (50g), finely chopped
2 tbsp finely chopped coriander (cilantro)
1 tbsp lime juice
1 tbsp extra virgin olive oil
2 Little Gem lettuce, torn

1 Combine chicken, taco seasoning, Cheddar and ⅓ cup (80ml) of the taco sauce in a bowl; season with salt and pepper to taste. Divide chicken mixture among tortillas, placing along the centre of each one; flatten chicken mixture slightly and shape into a rectangle. Fold in ends of tortillas, then roll up to enclose the filling; spray all over with oil.

2 Preheat a 7-litre air fryer to 180°C/350°F for 3 minutes.

3 Taking care, place chimichangas, seam-side down, in the air-fryer basket; at 180°C/350°F, cook for 12 minutes, turning halfway through cooking time, until golden and filling is hot.

4 Meanwhile, to make avocado salsa, combine avocado, tomato, onion, coriander, lime juice and oil in a bowl; season with salt and pepper.

5 To serve, divide the chimichangas, lettuce and avocado salsa among plates; drizzle chimichangas with remaining taco sauce.

prep + cook time
45 minutes
serves 4

CRISP-SKINNED SALMON
WITH SALSA VERDE

---

4 x 185g (6oz) boneless salmon
   fillets, skin on
1 tbsp extra virgin olive oil
2 tsp sea salt flakes
1 small shallot, finely chopped
1 garlic clove, crushed
2 tsp finely grated lemon zest
2 tbsp lemon juice
2 tbsp finely chopped dill
¼ cup (10g) chopped
   flat-leaf parsley
2 tbsp chopped chives
1 tbsp baby capers,
   coarsely chopped
to serve: extra sea salt flakes

1 Preheat a 7-litre air fryer to 200°C/400°F for 3 minutes.
2 Rub salmon with oil, then sprinkle with sea salt flakes.
3 Taking care, line the air-fryer basket with a silicone mat, if available (see page 11). Place salmon, skin-side up, in the basket; at 200°C/400°F, cook for 8 minutes until skin is crisp and salmon is cooked to your liking.

4 Meanwhile, to make salsa verde, combine remaining ingredients in a medium bowl, then season with salt and pepper; mix well.
5 Serve salmon topped with salsa verde and sprinkled with extra sea salt flakes.

MATCH IT Mustard & Mint Potatoes, page 145.

**prep + cook time
25 minutes serves 4**

PEPPERONI CALZONES

200g (6½oz) piece of pepperoni, thinly sliced
1 medium red pepper (200g), deseeded, thinly sliced
250g (8oz) frozen chopped spinach, thawed
⅓ cup (50g) semi-dried tomato strips, without oil
2 tbsp chopped oregano
⅔ cup (70g) coarsely grated mozzarella
2 x 250g (8oz) fresh pizza dough balls (see tip on page 60)
¼ cup (65g) thick pizza sauce (tomato purée with herbs)
to serve: sea salt flakes

1 Heat a large non-stick frying pan over a medium-high heat; cook pepperoni and red pepper, stirring, for 5 minutes or until golden and tender. Transfer to a plate lined with kitchen paper to cool.

2 Meanwhile, squeeze spinach to remove any excess liquid; transfer to a medium bowl. Add pepperoni mixture, semi-dried tomato strips, oregano and mozzarella; stir to combine.

3 Divide each dough ball into two even pieces. Roll out dough portions on a piece of lightly floured baking parchment into 18cm (7¼in) rounds. Spread dough rounds evenly with pizza sauce, leaving a 1.5cm (¾in) border around the edge. Top half of each dough round with pepperoni filling mixture, then fold dough over to enclose filling;

pinch edges to seal, then fold edges over themselves to pleat. Using a small, sharp knife, make three cuts in the tops. Trim the baking parchment so that it is 3cm (1¼in) larger all around than two of the calzones together.

4 Preheat a 7-litre air fryer to 180°C/350°F for 3 minutes.

5 Taking care, and using the parchment as an aid, lower the two calzones into the air-fryer basket; at 180°C/350°F, cook for 14 minutes, turning halfway through cooking time, or until crust is golden and calzones are cooked through. Transfer to a plate; cover to keep warm. Repeat cooking with remaining calzones.

6 Sprinkle calzones with sea salt flakes to serve.

**prep + cook time
45 minutes serves 4**

PICK-A-SAUCE

GREEN OLIVE DRESSING

prep time 5 minutes makes ¾ cup (185ml)
Process ½ cup pitted Sicilian green (nocellara) olives, 2 tbsp
oregano leaves and ⅓ cup (80ml) olive oil until almost smooth;
season with salt and pepper to taste.

FETA DRESSING

prep time 5 minutes makes 1 cup (250ml)
Process ½ cup (130g) Greek-style yogurt, 100g (3oz)
crumbled feta and 2 tbsp lime juice until smooth; season with
salt and pepper to taste. Stir in 1 tsp finely grated lime zest.

MISO AVOCADO DRESSING

prep time 5 minutes makes ¾ cup (185ml)
Process 1 chopped medium avocado (250g), 3 tsp white miso
paste (shiro miso) and ¼ cup (75g) mayonnaise until smooth;
season with salt and pepper to taste.

CHILLI & LIME MAYO

prep time 5 minutes makes about 1½ cups (325g)
Combine 1 cup (235g) mayonnaise with ¼ cup (60ml) sriracha
chilli sauce and 2 tbsp lime juice in a small bowl.

CHILLI PEANUT DRESSING

prep time 10 minutes makes ¾ cup (185ml)
Process 1 crushed garlic clove, 1 finely chopped long
red chilli, ⅓ cup (50g) roasted unsalted peanuts, ¼ cup (60ml)
fresh lime juice, the roots from 1 bunch of coriander (cilantro),
2 tbsp light soft brown sugar, 1 tbsp soy sauce and 1 tbsp
water until peanuts are finely chopped and ingredients
are combined.

CHIMICHURRI

prep time 5 minutes makes 1¼ cups (310ml)
Blend or process 2 tbsp red wine vinegar, ½ cup (125ml) extra
virgin olive oil, 4 finely chopped garlic cloves, ½ tsp dried
chilli flakes, 1 tsp sea salt flakes, 2 cups (40g) flat-leaf parsley
leaves and 2 tbsp oregano leaves until finely chopped.

ITALIAN CHICKEN RISSOLES

500g (1lb) chicken mince (ground chicken)
1 egg
2 tbsp pine nuts, lightly toasted
¼ cup (15g) finely chopped basil
1 garlic clove, crushed
60g (2oz) semi-dried tomatoes, chopped
1 cup (75g) panko breadcrumbs
8 thin slices of prosciutto (60g), halved lengthways
olive oil cooking spray
1 bunch (125g) of rocket (arugula), trimmed
1 tbsp extra virgin olive oil
1 tbsp balsamic vinegar
2 tbsp shaved Parmesan

1 Combine chicken, egg, pine nuts, basil, garlic, semi-dried tomatoes and half of the breadcrumbs in a medium bowl, then season with salt and pepper; mix well. Shape mixture into eight 2cm-thick rissoles. Roll rissoles in remaining breadcrumbs to coat lightly. Wrap one strip of prosciutto around each rissole, then another to make a cross shape, twisting ends to secure; lightly spray all over with oil.
2 Preheat a 7-litre air fryer to 180°C/350°F for 3 minutes.

3 Spray the air-fryer basket with oil. Taking care, place the rissoles in the basket; at 180°C/350°F, cook for 8 minutes, turning halfway through cooking time, or until browned and cooked through.
4 Meanwhile, place rocket, oil, vinegar and Parmesan in a medium bowl; toss gently to combine.
5 Serve rissoles with rocket salad.

**prep + cook time
30 minutes serves 4**

SPICED PRAWN PO' BOYS

2 eggs
¾ cup (55g) panko breadcrumbs
1 tbsp Cajun seasoning
16 uncooked prawns (shrimp),
   peeled, deveined
olive oil cooking spray
1 long baguette
⅓ cup (100g) mayonnaise
1 Little Gem lettuce (180g),
   leaves separated
2 medium tomatoes (300g),
   thinly sliced
3 gherkins, cut into rounds
to serve: extra mayonnaise, chopped
   chives and extra gherkins

1 Lightly beat eggs and 1 tablespoon water in a shallow bowl. Combine breadcrumbs and Cajun seasoning in a second shallow bowl. Dip prawns in egg, then coat in breadcrumb mixture; spray generously all over with oil.
2 Preheat a 7-litre air fryer to 180°C/350°F for 3 minutes.
3 Taking care, place prawns in the air-fryer basket in a single layer; at 180°C/350°F, cook for 6 minutes, turning halfway through cooking time, until golden brown and cooked through.

4 Trim ends from baguette and discard; cut baguette into four even pieces, then split horizontally, being careful not to cut all the way through. Spread bases with mayonnaise, then fill with lettuce, tomato, gherkins and prawns; drizzle with extra mayonnaise and sprinkle over chopped chives. Serve with extra gherkins.

**prep + cook time
35 minutes serves 4**

CLASSIC MEATBALLS

2 slices of white bread (90g)
⅓ cup (80ml) milk
1 medium onion (150g),
   coarsely grated
2 garlic cloves, crushed
1 medium carrot (120g),
   finely grated
750g (1½lb) beef mince
   (ground beef)
¼ cup (7g) chopped flat-leaf parsley
1 egg, lightly beaten
2 tbsp tomato purée
olive oil cooking spray
1½ cups (420g) tomato passata
400g (12½oz) jar olive pasta sauce
to serve: lasagnette (or spaghetti),
   grated Parmesan and basil leaves

1 Tear bread into a large bowl; pour over milk. Add onion, garlic, carrot, beef, parsley, egg and tomato purée; season well. Allow to stand for 10 minutes without stirring.

2 Preheat a 5.3-litre air fryer to 200°C/400°F for 5 minutes.

3 Using your hands, combine ingredients well in the bowl. With damp hands, shape 1½ tablespoons of the mince mixture into balls; spray with oil.

4 Spray the air-fryer basket with oil. Taking care, place half of the meatballs in the basket in a single layer; at 200°C/400°F, cook for 10 minutes, shaking basket halfway through cooking time, until browned and cooked through. Transfer to a tray; cover to keep warm. Repeat cooking with remaining meatballs.

5 Combine passata and pasta sauce in a bowl. Roll meatballs in tomato sauce mixture; place in a 15cm x 22cm (6in x 8¾in), 1.5-litre (6-cup) oval heatproof dish. Pour remaining tomato sauce mixture over meatballs. Place dish in the basket; at 200°C/400°F, cook for 10 minutes until heated through.

6 Serve lasagnette topped with meatballs and sauce, grated Parmesan and basil leaves.

OTHER FLAVOURS
Greek lamb meatballs
Swap beef mince for lamb mince and parsley for oregano. Add 2 teaspoons ground cinnamon and ½ teaspoon chilli flakes to tomato sauce mixture in step 5. Serve with orzo (risoni), Greek-style yogurt and pine nuts.
Mexican stuffed meatballs Add 2 teaspoons ground cumin and 1 teaspoon Tabasco chipotle sauce to meatball mixture in step 1. Combine 150g (4½oz) each of grated mozzarella and Cheddar; roll into small balls and press into the centre of each meatball in step 3.

prep + cook time
45 minutes serves 6

PREP IT The chicken can be prepared to the end of step 2 up to 4 hours ahead; refrigerate until needed.

CRUMBED CHICKEN
WITH SPICY MAYO

½ cup (75g) plain (all-purpose) flour
2 eggs
1 cup (75g) panko breadcrumbs
½ cup (40g) finely grated Parmesan
¼ cup (7g) coarsely chopped
   flat-leaf parsley
2 tsp finely grated lemon zest
12 skinless boneless chicken mini
   breast fillets (chicken tenders)
   (900g)
olive oil cooking spray
3 cups (75g) mixed salad leaves
2 tsp lemon juice
to serve: lemon wedges

SPICY MAYONNAISE
⅔ cup (200g) mayonnaise
¾ tsp peri-peri seasoning
2 tsp lemon juice

1 Preheat a 5.3-litre air fryer to 180°C/350°F for 3 minutes.
2 Place flour in a shallow bowl; season with salt and freshly ground black pepper. Lightly beat eggs in a second shallow bowl. Combine breadcrumbs, Parmesan, parsley and lemon zest in a third shallow bowl. Dust chicken in flour, shaking off excess, dip in egg, then coat in breadcrumb mixture; spray generously with oil.
3 Taking care, place chicken in the air-fryer basket; at 180°C/350°F, cook for 8 minutes, turning halfway through cooking time, or until golden and cooked through.

4 Meanwhile, to make spicy mayonnaise, combine ingredients in a small bowl.
5 Place salad leaves in a medium bowl with lemon juice; toss to combine.
6 Serve crumbed chicken with spicy mayonnaise, salad leaves and lemon wedges.

**prep + cook time
25 minutes serves 4**

83

LEMON & GARLIC ROAST CHICKEN

60g (2oz) butter, softened
1 garlic clove, crushed
1 tsp sweet paprika
2 tsp chopped rosemary
1 tsp chopped thyme
1 whole chicken, about 1.2kg (2½lb)
½ medium lemon (70g), halved
8 sprigs of lemon thyme
cooking oil spray
1 garlic bulb, halved crossways
4 sprigs of bay leaves
1 cup (250ml) gravy, warmed

1 Preheat a 5.3-litre air fryer to 160°C/325°F for 3 minutes.
2 Combine butter, garlic, paprika, rosemary and thyme in a small bowl.
3 Remove and discard any fat from cavity of chicken. Pat the cavity and skin dry with kitchen paper. Tuck wings under body. Run your fingers carefully between the skin and the breast meat. Push butter mixture under skin to cover breast. Fill cavity of chicken with lemon and half of the lemon thyme sprigs. Tie legs together with kitchen string.
4 Spray the air-fryer basket with oil. Taking care, place chicken in the basket and cover loosely with foil; at 160°C/325°F, cook for 30 minutes.

5 Uncover chicken and place garlic bulb halves and bay leaves beside it; at 160°C/325°F, cook for a further 30 minutes until juices run clear when a skewer is inserted into the thickest part of a thigh. Transfer chicken, garlic and bay leaves to a serving dish or platter; allow to stand for 10 minutes.
6 Serve chicken with the bay leaves, garlic, remaining lemon thyme sprigs and warm gravy.

prep + cook time
1¼ hours serves 4

PREP IT Patties can
be prepared a day
ahead; refrigerate
until needed. Brush
with barbecue sauce
before cooking.

LOADED KOREAN BURGER
WITH KIMCHI SLAW

1 tbsp light soft brown sugar

2 tbsp soy sauce

¼ cup (85g) gochujang chilli paste
   (see tips)

2 garlic cloves, crushed

2 tsp finely grated fresh root ginger

700g (1½lb) beef mince
   (ground beef)

1 egg

¾ cup (75g) packaged breadcrumbs

2 tbsp barbecue sauce

cooking oil spray

4 slices of Cheddar (160g)

4 large brioche buns (400g)

⅓ cup (100g) Japanese mayonnaise

to serve: sweet potato chips

KIMCHI SLAW

¼ cup (25g) kimchi, finely shredded

2 tsp rice wine vinegar

2 tsp vegetable oil

2 tsp sesame oil

2 cups (160g) shredded cabbage
   (see tips)

⅓ cup (7g) mint leaves

1 Preheat a 5.3-litre air fryer to 180°C/350°F for 3 minutes.

2 Combine sugar, soy sauce, all but 1 teaspoon of the chilli paste, the garlic and ginger in a bowl. Add beef, egg and breadcrumbs; using your hands, combine well. Shape mixture into four patties the same size as the brioche buns; ensure that they will all fit in the air-fryer basket. Brush all over with barbecue sauce.

3 Spray the air-fryer basket with oil. Taking care, place patties in the basket; at 180°C/350°F, cook for 6 minutes, turning halfway through cooking time, or until browned and cooked through. Top each one with a slice of Cheddar. Slide air-fryer pan and basket back into appliance. With air fryer turned off, leave patties for 1 minute for Cheddar to melt.

4 Meanwhile, to make kimchi slaw, combine kimchi, vinegar and oils in a large bowl. Add cabbage and mint to bowl; toss to combine.

5 Split and toast brioche buns. Spread bases with combined mayonnaise and remaining 1 teaspoon chilli paste, then top with patties and slaw; sandwich together with bun tops.

6 Serve burgers with sweet potato chips or fries.

TIPS Gochujang is a Korean fermented red chilli paste, available in major supermarkets and Asian grocers. Substitute with your favourite chilli sauce, if you like, adjusting the amount to your heat tolerance and palate. We used a mix of shredded red cabbage and Chinese leaf (napa cabbage); however, you can use any cabbage mix you like, including undressed coleslaw-type mixes.

**prep + cook time
30 minutes makes 4**

PORTUGUESE CHICKEN DRUMSTICKS

2 garlic cloves, chopped
1 long red chilli, chopped
1 tbsp finely chopped oregano
2 tbsp apple cider vinegar
1 tbsp extra virgin olive oil
1 tbsp light soft brown sugar
2 tsp smoked paprika
1 tsp sea salt flakes
8 chicken drumsticks (1.2kg)

1 To make marinade, place garlic, chilli and oregano in a small food processor or blender; blend until finely chopped. Add vinegar, oil, sugar, paprika and salt; process until combined.

2 Place chicken in a large shallow dish; add marinade and toss to coat. Cover with cling film. Refrigerate for 2 hours.

3 Preheat a 7-litre air fryer to 200°C/400°F for 3 minutes.

4 Taking care, place drained chicken (see tip, right) in the air-fryer basket; at 200°C/400°F, cook for 25 minutes, turning halfway through cooking time, or until cooked through.

TIP Heat drained marinade in a small saucepan for 3 minutes until reduced and slightly thickened, then use to baste the chicken while cooking.

**prep + cook time
40 minutes
(+ refrigeration)
serves 4**

VEGGIES
& SIDES

The air fryer can make your side dishes the stars of the meal. Think warm veg salads, jacket potatoes, loaded corn, mac 'n' cheese croquettes, crisp tofu with Asian-style dressing, carrot rösti and more.

CAJUN SWEET POTATO WEDGES

2 tsp ground cumin
1 tsp ground coriander
1 tsp garlic salt
½ tsp smoked paprika
½ tsp dried thyme
½ tsp dried oregano
½ tsp cayenne pepper
1kg (2lb) small sweet potatoes
1 tbsp extra virgin olive oil
to serve: sea salt flakes,
    chopped coriander (cilantro)
    and soured cream

1 Preheat a 7-litre air fryer to 200°C/400°F for 3 minutes.
2 To make Cajun spice mix, combine cumin, coriander, garlic salt, paprika, thyme, oregano and cayenne pepper in a small bowl.
3 Scrub sweet potatoes and pat dry; cut into long, thin wedges. Place in a large bowl with oil and the Cajun spice mix; toss to coat evenly.
4 Taking care, place wedges in the air-fryer basket; at 200°C/400°F, cook for 15 minutes, turning halfway through cooking time, or until golden and cooked through.

5 Sprinkle wedges with sea salt flakes and chopped coriander. Serve with soured cream.

**prep + cook time
25 minutes serves 4**

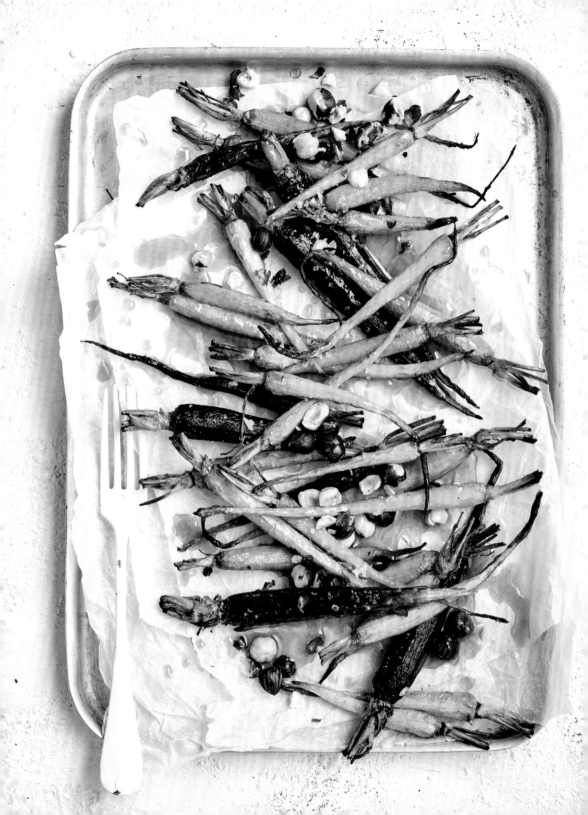

MAPLE-ROASTED CARROTS
WITH HAZELNUTS

2–3 bunches of baby rainbow
   carrots (500g in total), peeled
20g (¾oz) butter, melted
1 tbsp extra virgin olive oil
2 tbsp maple syrup
1 garlic clove, crushed
¼ cup (35g) unroasted hazelnuts

1 Preheat a 7-litre air fryer to 200°C/400°F for 3 minutes.
2 Cut any large carrots in half lengthways. Place carrots in a large bowl with butter, oil, maple syrup and garlic, then season with salt and freshly ground black pepper; toss to combine.
3 Taking care, place carrots in the air-fryer basket, reserving any leftover butter mixture in the bowl; at 200°C/400°F, cook for 10 minutes, turning halfway through cooking time.

4 Scatter hazelnuts over carrots; at 200°C/400°F, cook for a further 5 minutes or until carrots are golden and tender.
5 To serve, drizzle carrots and hazelnuts with reserved butter mixture.

**prep + cook time
25 minutes serves 4**

SALT 'N' VINEGAR SMASHED POTATOES

1.2kg (2½lb) red potatoes such as Desiree, Pontiac, Red Lady or Red King Edward, halved if large
3 cups (750ml) white vinegar
1 tbsp cooking salt
¼ cup (60ml) extra virgin olive oil
1 garlic bulb, cloves separated but unpeeled
1 bunch (20g) of rosemary sprigs

1 Place potatoes in a large saucepan. Add vinegar, cooking salt and enough water to just cover; bring to the boil. Boil, partially covered, for 15–20 minutes (the cooking time will vary depending on the size of the potatoes) or until potatoes are tender; drain.

2 Preheat a 5.3-litre air fryer to 200°C/400°F for 3 minutes.

3 Transfer potatoes to a large baking tray. Using a potato masher or the back of a spoon, press down on potatoes until flattened slightly and skins split. Brush potatoes with oil.

4 Taking care, place potatoes in the air-fryer basket; at 200°C/400°F, cook for 30 minutes, turning twice during cooking time, or until potatoes are golden. Add garlic 10 minutes into cooking time and rosemary in the last 5 minutes.

5 Season smashed potatoes generously with sea salt. Serve with roast garlic and rosemary sprigs.

**prep + cook time
55 minutes serves 6**

SIDE SALADS

ITALIAN-STYLE RICE SALAD

Heat a 450g (14½oz) packet microwaveable brown rice according to packet directions; transfer to a large bowl. Add ½ cup (75g) semi-dried tomato strips (not in oil), ⅓ cup (15g) basil leaves, 60g (2oz) coarsely chopped baby spinach, ⅔ cup (80g) sliced pitted Sicilian green (nocellara) olives, 1 thinly sliced small red onion and ¼ cup (60ml) balsamic dressing. Season to taste. Toss gently to combine.

EDAMAME SLAW

Place 2 cups (160g) finely shredded red cabbage, 150g (4½oz) shredded carrot, ½ cup (70g) unsalted roasted peanuts, 1 finely chopped long red chilli, 400g (12½oz) peeled and blanched edamame and ½ cup (125ml) Asian-style sesame, soy and ginger dressing in a large bowl. Season to taste. Toss gently to combine.

LENTIL TABBOULEH

Place 2 x 420g (13½oz) cans drained lentils, 1 cup (20g) each of small flat-leaf parsley and mint leaves, 4 sliced spring onions (scallions), 250g (4oz) sliced heirloom cherry tomatoes, ¼ cup (60ml) lemon juice and ¼ cup (60ml) olive oil in a large bowl. Season to taste. Toss gently to combine.

KALE, PEAR, SMOKED CHEDDAR & ALMOND SALAD

Place 60g (2oz) chopped kale, 1 medium cored and thinly sliced pear, ⅓ cup (40g) finely grated smoked Cheddar, ¼ cup (40g) chopped roasted almonds, 2 tbsp lemon juice and 1 tbsp olive oil in a large bowl. Season to taste. Toss gently to combine.

4 WAYS

ITALIAN-STYLE
RICE SALAD

LENTIL
TABBOULEH

EDAMAME
SLAW

KALE, PEAR,
SMOKED
CHEDDAR &
ALMOND SALAD

BRUSSELS SPROUTS REVOLUTION

300g (9½oz) broccoli

300g (9½oz) baby red and green Brussels sprouts

240g (7½oz) kale, stems removed and discarded

2 tbsp extra virgin olive oil

2 tbsp honey

cooking oil spray

2 garlic cloves, thinly sliced

75g (2½oz) prosciutto

⅓ cup (80g) chopped roasted almonds

GREEN TAHINI

2 tbsp tahini

2 tbsp lemon juice

2 tbsp cold water

1 tbsp extra virgin olive oil

⅓ cup (15g) baby spinach leaves

1 Preheat a 5.3-litre air fryer to 200°C/400°F for 3 minutes.

2 Cut broccoli into florets. Trim base and remove tough outer leaves from Brussels sprouts. Tear leaves from kale into smaller pieces.

3 Combine olive oil and honey in a medium bowl. Add broccoli and Brussels sprouts; toss to coat. Season to taste.

4 Taking care, place broccoli mixture in the air-fryer basket; at 200°C/400°F, cook for 8 minutes, stirring halfway through cooking time, or until vegetables are beginning to crisp at edges.

5 Place kale leaves in the basket and spray with oil; at 200°C/400°F, cook for 4 minutes.

6 Place garlic and prosciutto on top of vegetables; at 200°C/400°F, cook for 5 minutes until prosciutto is crisp.

7 Meanwhile, to make green tahini, process ingredients until smooth; season to taste. Add a little more water, if needed, to achieve a drizzling consistency.

8 Serve sprouts mixture with crumbled prosciutto, drizzled with green tahini and topped with almonds.

**prep + cook time
35 minutes serves 4**

GOLDEN ONION RINGS

¼ cup (35g) plain (all-purpose) flour
1 tsp smoked paprika
1 egg
1 tbsp cold water
1½ cups (110g) panko breadcrumbs
2 medium onions (300g), cut into
  1cm (½in) slices, separated
  into rings
olive oil cooking spray
to serve: aïoli

1 Combine flour and paprika in a shallow bowl; season with salt and freshly ground black pepper. Lightly beat egg and the cold water in a second shallow bowl. Place breadcrumbs in a third shallow bowl. Dust onion rings in flour mixture, shaking off excess, dip in egg, then coat in breadcrumbs; spray generously all over with oil.
2 Preheat a 7-litre air fryer to 190°C/375°F for 3 minutes.
3 Taking care, place half of the onion rings in the air-fryer basket; at 190°C/375°F, cook for 5 minutes or until golden and tender. Transfer to a wire rack. Repeat cooking with remaining onion rings.
4 Serve onion rings with aïoli.

**prep + cook time
25 minutes serves 4**

VEGGIE MAC 'N' CHEESE CROQUETTES

You will need to start this recipe
   a day ahead.
1⅓ cups (240g) macaroni
1 medium courgette (zucchini)
   (120g), finely chopped
1 cup (140g) frozen garden peas
   and sweetcorn
50g (1¾oz) butter
1⅓ cups (200g) plain (all-
   purpose) flour
2 cups (500ml) milk
1 tsp Dijon mustard
2 spring onions (scallions),
   thinly sliced
1 small red pepper (150g),
   finely chopped
½ cup (60g) grated mozzarella
¼ cup (30g) grated Cheddar
¼ cup (20g) grated Parmesan
2 eggs
2 cups (150g) panko breadcrumbs
¼ cup finely chopped chives
olive oil cooking spray
to serve: sea salt flakes and
   tomato chutney

1 Grease a 20cm x 30cm (8in x 12in) traybake tin; line bottom and sides with baking parchment, extending parchment 5cm (2in) over edges.

2 Cook pasta in a large saucepan of boiling salted water according to the packet directions, adding courgette and frozen peas and sweetcorn for the last 3 minutes of cooking time; drain well. Return pasta and vegetables to pan.

3 Meanwhile, make cheese sauce. Melt butter in a medium saucepan over a medium-high heat. Add ⅓ cup (50g) of the flour; cook, stirring, for 2 minutes or until bubbling. Gradually stir in milk; cook, stirring, for 5 minutes or until sauce boils and thickens. Remove from heat; stir in mustard, spring onions, red pepper and cheeses until cheese is melted.

4 Pour cheese sauce over pasta and vegetables in pan; stir to combine. Spoon pasta mixture into traybake tin; smooth the surface. Refrigerate for 6 hours or overnight until firm.

5 Turn firm pasta mixture onto a clean work surface; cut into 4cm pieces. Put remaining flour in a shallow bowl. Lightly whisk eggs in a second shallow bowl. Mix breadcrumbs and chives in a third shallow bowl. Dust pasta pieces in flour, shaking off excess, dip in egg, then coat in breadcrumb mixture; place on a tray. Refrigerate for 15 minutes.

6 Preheat a 7-litre air fryer to 200°C/400°F for 3 minutes.

7 Spray croquettes generously all over with oil. Taking care, place half of the croquettes in the air-fryer basket in a single layer; at 200°C/400°F, cook for 10 minutes, turning halfway through cooking time, or until crisp and golden. Using a spatula or slotted turner, carefully transfer to a plate; cover loosely with foil to keep warm. Repeat cooking with remaining croquettes.

8 Sprinkle croquettes with sea salt flakes and serve with tomato chutney.

**prep + cook time
50 minutes
(+ refrigeration)
serves 4**

ROASTED SQUASH
WITH PEPITA SALSA

1kg (2lb) kabocha squash such as
Kent, unpeeled, cut into 3cm
(1¼in) thick wedges
2 tbsp extra virgin olive oil
¼ cup (50g) pumpkin seeds
(pepitas), toasted
250g (8oz) feta, crumbled
to serve: flat-leaf parsley leaves

PEPITA SALSA
½ cup (100g) pumpkin seeds
(pepitas), toasted
1 cup (20g) flat-leaf parsley leaves
½ cup (125ml) extra virgin olive oil
⅓ cup (80ml) lime juice
1 small garlic clove, crushed

1 Preheat a 5.3-litre air
fryer to 200°C/400°F for
3 minutes.
2 Place squash wedges
and oil in a large bowl;
season with salt and
freshly ground black
pepper. Using your fingers,
massage the oil onto each
squash wedge.
3 Taking care, place
pumpkin upright in the
air-fryer basket; at
200°C/400°F, cook for
40 minutes, turning a
number of times during
cooking time, until tender.
4 Meanwhile, to make
pepita salsa, process
ingredients until mixture
forms a slightly chunky
salsa; season to taste.

5 Serve pumpkin wedges
topped with pepita salsa,
toasted pumpkin seeds,
feta and parsley leaves.

PREP IT Pepita
salsa can be made
up to 4 days ahead;
refrigerate in a
screw-top jar, covered
with a thin layer of
extra virgin olive oil,
until needed.

**prep + cook time 1 hour
serves 6**

POTATO GRATIN

750g (1½lb) floury potatoes
   such as King Edward, Maris Piper
   or russet, peeled
⅔ cup (160ml) single (light) cream,
   warmed
⅓ cup (80ml) milk, warmed
2 garlic cloves, crushed
1 tbsp rosemary leaves
1 small onion (80g), thinly sliced
1 cup (120g) grated Gruyère cheese
to serve: sea salt flakes

1 Using a mandolin, V-slicer or sharp knife, slice potatoes very thinly.
2 Whisk cream, milk, garlic and rosemary in a large jug until combined; season with salt and freshly ground black pepper.
3 Layer potato slices, onion and cream mixture in a 20cm (8in) round ovenproof dish, finishing with the cream mixture. Using your hands, press down firmly on the potatoes.
4 Preheat a 7-litre air fryer to 160°C/325°F for 3 minutes.
5 Taking care, place the dish in the air-fryer basket; at 160°C/325°F, cook for 25 minutes until potatoes are just tender.
6 Scatter potatoes with Gruyère; at 160°C/325°F, cook potato gratin for a further 5 minutes or until cheese is golden.
7 Sprinkle gratin with sea salt flakes to serve.

**prep + cook time
45 minutes serves 6**

109

LOADED SWEETCORN

6 sweetcorn cobs (1.5kg), in husks
100g (3oz) fresh goat's cheese,
  crumbled
finely grated zest of 1 lime
¼ cup (7g) coriander
  (cilantro) leaves
¼ cup (20g) Asian fried shallots
to serve: lime wedges

SRIRACHA & LIME BUTTER
125g (4oz) butter, chopped, softened
¼ cup (70g) sriracha chilli sauce
2 tsp lime juice

1 Cook sweetcorn cobs in their husks in a large saucepan of boiling salted water for 3 minutes or until almost tender; drain. Allow to cool. Peel back husks; remove and discard silks. Tie the husks back with kitchen string.
2 Preheat a 5.3-litre air fryer to 200°C/400°F for 3 minutes.
3 Bend husks back so that sweetcorn will fit in the air-fryer basket; wrap just the husks of each cob in foil to prevent burning.
4 Taking care, place half of the sweetcorn cobs in the air-fryer basket; at 200°C/400°F, cook for 10 minutes. Transfer to a plate; cover to keep warm. Repeat cooking with remaining sweetcorn cobs.

5 Meanwhile, to make sriracha and lime butter, process butter in a small food processor until whipped. Add sriracha and lime juice; process until smooth.
6 Spread sriracha and lime butter on hot sweetcorn; top with goat's cheese, lime zest, coriander and fried shallots. Serve with lime wedges.

**prep + cook time
35 minutes makes 6**

ASPARAGUS WITH PROSCIUTTO
& GARLIC BUTTER

24 asparagus spears (600g),
    trimmed
4 slices of prosciutto (60g),
    halved lengthways
olive oil cooking spray
30g (1oz) butter
1 garlic clove, crushed
2 tsp thyme leaves

1 Preheat a 7-litre air fryer to 180°C/350°F for 3 minutes.
2 Group asparagus into bundles of three spears each. Wrap a slice of prosciutto around each bundle to secure; spray all over with oil.
3 Taking care, place asparagus bundles in the air-fryer basket; at 180°C/350°F, cook for 6 minutes, turning halfway through cooking time, until prosciutto is golden and asparagus is tender.

4 Meanwhile, to make garlic butter, cook butter and garlic in a small frying pan over a medium heat until butter is melted; stir in thyme. Season with salt and freshly ground black pepper.
5 Serve asparagus bundles drizzled with garlic butter.

**prep + cook time
15 minutes serves 4**

HASSELBACK SWEET POTATOES

6 mini orange sweet potatoes
    (1.2kg)
60g (2oz) butter, melted
2 garlic cloves, crushed
½ tsp ground cinnamon
2 tsp sea salt flakes
100g (3oz) sliced round mild
    pancetta (use smoked pancetta
    slices if can't find rolled pancetta)
1 tbsp chopped chives

WHIPPED CHIVE BUTTER
80g (2½oz) butter, softened
1 tsp maple syrup
2 tbsp chopped chives

1 Wash unpeeled sweet potatoes; place on a chopping board. Trim a little piece lengthways from one side so that they sit flat. Place a chopstick on the board along each side of a sweet potato. Slice crossways at 1cm (½in) intervals, cutting through to the chopsticks (the chopsticks will prevent you from cutting all the way through). Repeat with remaining sweet potatoes.
2 Preheat a 5.3-litre air fryer to 200°C/400°F for 3 minutes.
3 Combine butter, garlic, cinnamon and sea salt flakes in a small bowl. Brush butter mixture over sweet potatoes.
4 Taking care, place sweet potatoes in the air-fryer basket; at 200°C/400°F, cook for 15 minutes.
5 Place pancetta on top of sweet potatoes; at 200°C/400°F, cook for

a further 5 minutes until sweet potatoes are tender when pierced with the tip of a knife and the pancetta is crisp.
6 Meanwhile, to make whipped chive butter, beat butter in a small bowl with an electric mixer until light and fluffy. Beat in maple syrup, then stir in chives.
7 Spread sweet potatoes with whipped chive butter. Serve topped with crisp pancetta and sprinkled with chopped chives.

SWAP IT You can use any type of sweet potato or even regular potatoes. If using regular potatoes, omit the cinnamon and use paprika instead. Regular potatoes will discolour when cut, so prepare close to serving.

prep + cook time 1 hour serves 6

PREP IT Sweet potatoes can be prepared to the end of step 3 up to 6 hours ahead; refrigerate until needed. Preheat the air fryer just before you're ready to cook.

SPICY CAJUN
POTATO WEDGES

PAPRIKA POTATO
WEDGES

SWEET
POTATO
WEDGES

LEMON PEPPER FRIES

CHILLI GARLIC FRIES

SALTED FRIES

SPICY CAJUN POTATO WEDGES

Preheat a 5.3-litre air fryer to 200°C/400°F for 3 minutes. Cut 1kg (2lb) unpeeled fingerling potatoes into wedges. Combine 2 tbsp olive oil, 2 tsp ground cumin, 1 tsp ground coriander, 1 tsp hot paprika, ½ tsp ground oregano, ½ tsp ground black pepper and ¼ tsp chilli powder in a large bowl. Add wedges and toss to coat. Place wedges in the air-fryer basket; cook for 15–20 minutes, turning once, until golden and cooked. Season with salt and serve topped with oregano leaves.

PAPRIKA POTATO WEDGES

Preheat a 5.3-litre air fryer to 200°C/400°F for 3 minutes. Cut 1kg (2lb) scrubbed floury potatoes such as Sebago or Maris Piper into wedges. Place in a large bowl with 2 tbsp extra virgin olive oil, 40g (1½oz) melted butter and 2 tsp smoked paprika. Season with salt and toss to coat. Place wedges in the air-fryer basket; cook for 15–20 minutes, turning once, until golden and cooked. Scatter with ½ cup (40g) finely grated Parmesan and serve with garlic mayonnaise.

6 WAYS HAND-CUT FRIES & WEDGES

SWEET POTATO WEDGES WITH CHILLI LIME SALT

Preheat a 5.3-litre air fryer to 200°C/400°F for 3 minutes. Cut 1kg (2lb) orange sweet potatoes into wedges. Toss with 2 tbsp olive oil. Place wedges in the air-fryer basket; cook for 15–20 minutes, turning once, or until golden and cooked. Combine 2 tsp finely grated lime zest, 2 tbsp sea salt flakes and 1 tsp chilli flakes in a small heatproof bowl; place in air fryer for the last 3 minutes of cooking time to dry out the zest. Sprinkle wedges with chilli lime salt to serve.

SALTED FRIES

Cut 1kg (2lb) peeled Russet Burbank or other floury potatoes lengthways into 1cm (½in) thick slices, then cut slices lengthways into 1cm (½in) thick batons. Place in a large bowl of cold water. Allow to stand for 30 minutes; drain, then pat dry with kitchen paper. Toss with 2 tbsp olive oil. Preheat a 5.3-litre air fryer to 200°C/400°F for 3 minutes. Place fries in the air-fryer basket; cook for 15–20 minutes, turning once, until golden and cooked. Season with salt.

LEMON PEPPER FRIES

Make a batch of Salted Fries (below left), omitting the salt. Combine 1 tbsp finely grated lemon zest, ½ tsp freshly ground black pepper and 1 tsp sea salt flakes in a small bowl. Sprinkle hot fries with lemon pepper and serve with lemon wedges.

swap it Use grated lime zest instead of lemon zest and crushed Sichuan peppercorns instead of black pepper.

serving suggestion These fries go well with battered or grilled fish, or with fish sandwiches, prawns (shrimp) and chicken.

CHILLI GARLIC FRIES

Make a batch of Salted Fries (left). Heat 2 tsp olive oil in a small frying pan. Cook 2 sliced long red chillies until soft. Add 2 sliced garlic cloves; cook, stirring, until fragrant. Sprinkle hot fries with chilli mixture to serve.

serving suggestion These fries go well with hamburgers, grilled or pan-fried steak, and lamb cutlets.

BEETROOT
WITH YOGURT & DUKKAH

700g (1½lb) mixed baby beetroot,
   scrubbed, unpeeled
   (see tip)
2 tbsp extra virgin olive oil
1½ tbsp dukkah spice mix
½ cup (140g) Greek-style yogurt
1 tbsp lemon juice
to serve: extra virgin olive oil and
   flat-leaf parsley leaves

1 Preheat a 7-litre air fryer to 180°C/350°F for 3 minutes.
2 Quarter, halve or cut beetroot into wedges so that all the pieces are a similar size. Place beetroot and oil in a large bowl; season. Using your fingers, massage the oil into each beetroot wedge (wear gloves if you don't want to stain your hands).
3 Taking care, place beetroot, cut-side up, in the air-fryer basket; at 180°C/350°F, cook for 25 minutes, turning a number of times, until tender. Scatter dukkah over beetroot for the last 5 minutes of cooking time.

4 Meanwhile, combine yogurt and lemon juice in a small bowl; season to taste.
5 To serve, spread yogurt mixture on a serving plate or platter; top with dukkah-spiced beetroot. Drizzle with extra olive oil and scatter with flat-leaf parsley leaves. Sprinkle with any dukkah that may have fallen through the basket holes into the pan.

**prep + cook time
35 minutes serves 4**

TIP You can also use
regular beetroot, cut into
1.5cm (¾in) wedges.

EPIC JACKET POTATOES

8 large all-purpose or floury
  potatoes or 4 small orange
  sweet potatoes (2.4kg)
extra virgin olive oil cooking spray
½ tsp sea salt flakes
to serve: butter

1 Preheat a 5.3-litre air fryer to 200°C/400°F for 3 minutes.
2 Prick potatoes all over with a fork. Taking care, place potatoes in the air-fryer basket, then spray with oil and sprinkle with salt flakes; at 200°C/400°F, cook for 40 minutes, turning halfway through cooking time, until tender when pierced with the tip of a knife.
3 Transfer potatoes to plates. Cut a cross in the top of each potato, then squeeze upwards from the bottom to open up. Serve with lashings of butter or with one of the toppers.

TOPPERS

nachos Heat a 425g (13½oz) can Mexe beans or refried whole pinto beans in a small saucepan. Top jacket potatoes with 25g (¾oz) tortilla chips, then the beans; scatter with 1 cup (120g) grated Cheddar. Return topped potatoes to the air-fryer basket; at 200°C/400°F, cook for 2 minutes until cheese melts. To serve, top potatoes with ½ cup (120g) soured cream, 1 fresh sliced jalapeño chilli and ¼ cup (7g) coriander (cilantro) leaves. Drizzle with your favourite chilli sauce. Season to taste.

baked barbecue beans Place 250g (8oz) halved cherry tomatoes in a medium saucepan with a 420g (13½oz) can baked beans, 1 tablespoon Dijon mustard and 1 tablespoon smoky barbecue sauce; cook over a medium heat, stirring occasionally, until mixture is heated through. To serve, top jacket potatoes with baked bean mixture and ¼ cup (20g) finely grated Parmesan. Season to taste.

TIP To reduce the air-fryer time, par-cook the potatoes first. Prick them all over with a fork, then microwave on HIGH (100%) for 8 minutes or until soft. Bake in the air fryer for 15 minutes.

**prep + cook time
45 minutes serves 4**

SESAME & CHILLI BROCCOLINI
WITH MUSHROOMS

2 bunches of broccolini (Tenderstem broccoli) (700g), trimmed
2 long red chillies, seeded, thickly sliced
200g (6½oz) mixed mushrooms, sliced (see tip)
1 tbsp sesame oil
3 garlic cloves, thinly sliced
1 tbsp sesame seeds
2 tbsp oyster sauce

1 Preheat a 7-litre air fryer to 180°C/350°F for 3 minutes.
2 Combine broccolini, chilli and mushrooms in a large bowl, then add sesame oil; toss to coat. Season with salt and freshly ground black pepper.
3 Taking care, place vegetable mixture in the air-fryer basket; at 180°C/350°F, cook for 10 minutes, tossing halfway through cooking time, or until vegetables are beginning to crisp at edges.
4 Sprinkle vegetables with garlic and sesame seeds; at 180°C/350°F, cook for a further 3 minutes until tender.
5 Serve vegetables drizzled with oyster sauce.

TIP We used shiitake, king oyster, oyster and button mushrooms.

**prep + cook time
25 minutes serves 4**

CARROT RÖSTI
WITH PARMESAN & THYME

2 medium carrots (240g),
  coarsely grated
1 medium floury or all-purpose
  potato (200g), coarsely grated
½ small onion (40g), coarsely grated
2 eggs, lightly beaten
½ cup (25g) finely grated Parmesan
1 tbsp cornflour (cornstarch)
1 tbsp finely chopped thyme leaves
1 garlic clove, crushed
olive oil cooking spray
to serve: sea salt flakes and
  soured cream

1 Preheat a 7-litre air fryer to 200°C/400°F for 3 minutes.
2 Combine carrot, potato, onion, egg, Parmesan, cornflour, thyme and garlic in a large bowl, then season; mix well. Shape carrot mixture into eight 1cm (½in) thick round rösti, pressing each firmly between hands to compact; spray all over with oil.
3 Spray the air-fryer basket with oil. Taking care, place rösti in the basket; at 180°C/350°F, cook for 14 minutes, turning halfway through cooking time, until golden and tender.
4 Sprinkle rösti with sea salt flakes and serve with soured cream.

**prep + cook time
35 minutes serves 4
(makes 8)**

CRISP TOFU
WITH PALM SUGAR DRESSING

600g (1lb) medium tofu
2 bunches of broccolini (Tenderstem broccoli) (700g), trimmed, thick stems halved lengthways
170g (5½oz) gai lan (Chinese broccoli), trimmed, cut into 5cm (2in) lengths
3 egg whites
1 cup (180g) rice flour
2 tbsp sesame seeds
1 tbsp ground white pepper
2 tsp freshly ground black pepper
2 tsp salt
olive oil cooking spray
to serve: sliced spring onions (scallions), sliced red chilli, extra sesame seeds and lime cheeks

PALM SUGAR DRESSING
1 tbsp finely grated fresh root ginger
¼ cup (60ml) extra virgin olive oil
2 tbsp lime juice
¼ cup (60ml) mirin
¼ cup (60ml) soy sauce
1 tbsp finely grated palm sugar
1 small red chilli, finely chopped

1 Cut tofu horizontally into four slices; cut each slice in half to make eight pieces in total. Line a chopping board with kitchen paper. Place tofu slices on kitchen paper; lay more kitchen paper on top of tofu, then top with a heavy tray (or small chopping board) to weigh down the tofu. Leave for 10 minutes to drain.

2 Preheat a 5.3-litre air fryer to 180°C/350°F for 3 minutes.

3 Rinse broccolini and gai lan. Taking care, place damp vegetables in the air-fryer basket; at 180°C/350°F, cook for 5 minutes until just tender. Transfer to a platter; cover to keep warm.

4 Meanwhile, to make palm sugar dressing, place ingredients in a screw-top jar; shake well to combine.

5 Beat egg whites in a shallow bowl. Combine rice flour, sesame seeds, white and black peppers and salt in a second shallow bowl. Dip tofu slices in egg white, then coat in rice flour mixture; spray generously with oil.

6 Place half of the tofu in the basket; at 180°C/350°F, cook for 15 minutes, turning halfway through cooking time, or until crisp and golden. Transfer to a wire rack. Repeat cooking with remaining tofu.

7 Top vegetables with crisp tofu, sliced spring onions, sliced chilli and extra sesame seeds; drizzle with dressing. Serve with lime cheeks.

**prep + cook time
45 minutes
serves 4**

WEEKENDS

The air fryer might be the best appliance for fast and easy cooking during the week, but it's also a superstar when it comes to cooking larger cuts of meat and fish, as well as more ambitious recipes.

STEAK
WITH BÉARNAISE & FRIES

600g (1½lb) potatoes, cut into 1cm
(½in) fries-style chips
olive oil cooking spray
4 x 200g (6½oz) beef rump
(top sirloin) steaks, about
(2cm/¾in) thick
2 cups (240g) frozen garden peas

BÉARNAISE SAUCE
½ cup (125ml) dry white wine
2 tbsp white wine vinegar
2 shallots (50g), finely chopped
1 tsp dried tarragon
1 tsp black peppercorns
3 egg yolks
250g (8oz) butter, melted
1 tbsp finely chopped fresh tarragon

1 To make Béarnaise sauce, combine wine, vinegar, shallots, dried tarragon and peppercorns in a small saucepan; simmer for 5 minutes or until liquid reduces to about 2 tablespoons. Strain through a fine sieve into a heatproof bowl; discard the shallot mixture. Place bowl containing wine mixture over a saucepan of simmering water (make sure the bowl doesn't touch the water). Add egg yolks to the bowl; whisk for 3 minutes or until the mixture is pale and frothy. Add butter, a tablespoon at a time, whisking continuously after each addition until sauce is thick and smooth. Remove from heat. Stir in fresh tarragon; season. Cover pan and set aside until needed.

2 Preheat an 11-litre air fryer to 200°C/400°F for 3 minutes.

3 Spray potato chips all over with oil; spread out on two of the air-fryer racks.

4 Taking care, slide the racks onto the lower shelves of the air fryer; at 200°C/400°F, cook for 20 minutes, rotating racks halfway through cooking time.

5 Place steaks on the remaining rack. Spray both sides with oil and season. Taking care, slide the rack into the second-highest shelf of the air fryer; at 200°C/400°F, cook for 7 minutes, turning after 2 minutes, or until steaks are medium or cooked to your liking and potato chips are golden and tender. Transfer steaks to a plate; cover loosely with foil and allow to rest for 5 minutes.

6 Meanwhile, boil, steam or microwave peas until just tender; drain.

7 Season steaks with freshly ground black pepper. Serve with Béarnaise sauce, chips and peas.

**prep + cook time 1 hour
serves 4**

TIPS Do not position the steaks on the highest shelf in the air fryer, as this can cause the appliance to smoke. For a smaller 7-litre air fryer, cook the potato chips first, then transfer to a plate while you cook the steaks. While the steaks are resting, reheat the chips in the air fryer.

MINI MEATLOAVES

WRAPPED IN MAPLE BACON

½ small onion (40g), finely grated
⅓ cup (10g) finely chopped
   flat-leaf parsley
2 garlic cloves, crushed
½ cup (50g) packaged breadcrumbs
1 egg, lightly beaten
¼ cup (70g) low-sugar
   tomato ketchup
1 tbsp Worcestershire sauce
500g (1lb) beef mince (ground beef)
1 tbsp chopped thyme leaves
4 rindless bacon rashers (250g)
½ tbsp maple syrup
to serve: extra low-sugar
   tomato ketchup

1 Preheat a 7-litre air fryer to 180°C/350°F for 3 minutes.
2 Combine onion, parsley, garlic, breadcrumbs, egg, tomato ketchup, Worcestershire sauce and beef in a large bowl, then season with salt and freshly ground black pepper; mix well to combine. Divide mixture into four even portions and shape each into a small loaf. Sprinkle with thyme, then wrap in bacon.
3 Taking care, place meatloaves, top-side down, in the air-fryer basket; at 180°C/350°F, cook for 20 minutes, turning halfway through cooking time. Brush tops with maple syrup during the last 5 minutes of cooking time.
4 Serve meatloaves with extra tomato ketchup.

SERVE IT Wrap meatloaves in cos (romaine) or iceberg lettuce leaves for a crunchy finish.

**prep + cook time
40 minutes serves 4**

MATCH IT Peri-Peri Potatoes, page 145.

SPICY KOREAN PEANUT PORK RIBS

2kg (4lb) American-style
    pork rib racks
2 garlic cloves, crushed
1 tsp finely grated fresh root ginger
¼ cup (95g) crunchy peanut butter
1 tbsp sriracha chilli sauce
1 tbsp soy sauce
2 tsp fish sauce
1 tbsp light soft brown sugar
2 tsp sesame oil
2 tbsp lime juice
½ cup (125ml) coconut cream
cooking oil spray
2 Lebanese cucumbers, seeded,
    halved lengthways, thinly sliced
2 long red chillies, finely chopped
to serve: lime wedges and
    steamed jasmine rice

1 Using a small, sharp knife, remove the layer of membrane from the back of the ribs (or ask your butcher to do this for you). Place ribs in a large saucepan and cover well with water; bring to the boil over a medium heat. Reduce heat; simmer for 45 minutes or until almost tender.

2 Meanwhile, to make marinade, put garlic, ginger, peanut butter, sauces, sugar, oil and half of the lime juice in a blender or small food processor; blend until smooth. Add coconut cream; blend until combined. Transfer to a large nonmetallic dish. Drain ribs; add to marinade and turn to coat. Cover. Refrigerate for 2 hours.

3 Preheat a 7-litre air fryer to 180°C/350°F for 3 minutes.

4 Spray the air-fryer basket with oil. Remove ribs from the marinade, scraping off any that has solidified; reserve remaining marinade. Taking care, arrange the ribs in the basket, standing them up and leaning them against the side of the basket and one another. Reset the temperature to 160°C/325°F; cook for 20 minutes.

5 Brush ribs with a third of the reserved marinade; at 160°C/325°F, cook for a further 10 minutes until tender and glazed.

6 Meanwhile, combine cucumber, chilli and remaining lime juice in a small bowl; season. Allow to stand for 10 minutes.

7 To make peanut sauce, place remaining reserved marinade and 2 tablespoons water in a small saucepan over a medium-high heat; bring to the boil. Reduce heat; simmer for 4 minutes or until thickened slightly.

8 Cut ribs into serving-sized pieces and place on a large platter; spoon over a little peanut sauce. Serve with remaining peanut sauce, the cucumber mixture, lime wedges and jasmine rice.

**prep + cook time
1 hour 40 minutes
(+ refrigeration)
serves 4**

CHICKEN & LEEK PIE

2 cups (500ml) chicken stock
625g (1¼lb) skinless boneless
   chicken breasts
2 sheets of frozen butter puff
   pastry, just thawed
1 egg, lightly beaten
cooking oil spray
60g (2oz) butter
1 large leek (500g), thinly sliced
2 celery sticks (300g), trimmed,
   finely chopped
2 tbsp plain (all-purpose) flour
2 tsp thyme leaves
½ cup (125ml) milk
1 cup (250ml) single (light) cream
2 tsp wholegrain mustard

1 Bring stock to the boil in a medium saucepan. Add chicken; return to the boil. Reduce heat; simmer, covered, for 10 minutes or until chicken is cooked through. Remove from heat. Allow chicken to stand in poaching liquid for 10 minutes.

2 Preheat a 5.3-litre air fryer to 180°C/350°F for 3 minutes.

3 Stack pastry sheets on top of one another. Place a 15cm x 22cm (6in x 8¾in), 1.5-litre (6-cup) rectangular dish over pastry stack; cut around it to cut out a rectangle the same size, then cut four slits crossways in the centre of the pastry. (Alternatively, use another-sized dish, but no larger than the pastry sheet.)

4 Brush pastry with egg. Spray the air-fryer basket with oil. Taking care, place pastry stack in the basket; at 180°C/350°F, cook for 15–18 minutes until pastry is puffed and deep golden.

5 Meanwhile, remove chicken from liquid; coarsely chop. Reserve 1 cup (250ml) of the poaching liquid. (Keep remaining liquid for another use or discard.) Heat butter in a medium saucepan; cook leek and celery, stirring, until leek softens. Add flour and thyme; cook, stirring, for 1 minute. Gradually stir in reserved poaching liquid, the milk and cream; cook, stirring, until mixture boils and thickens. Stir in chopped chicken and the mustard. Season to taste.

6 Spoon hot chicken mixture into dish; carefully place cooked puff pastry on top. Serve pie scattered with extra thyme, if you like.

prep + cook time
45 minutes serves 6

PREP IT Pie filling can
be made a day ahead;
refrigerate until needed.

BUTTERFLIED HARISSA CHICKEN
WITH COUSCOUS & ORANGE

1 whole chicken, about 1.4kg (2¾lb)
2 garlic cloves, crushed
2 tbsp lemon juice
2 tsp sweet paprika
1 tbsp harissa paste (see tip)
2 tbsp extra virgin olive oil
olive oil cooking spray
1 cup (200g) couscous
1 cup (250ml) boiling water
½ cup (15g) coriander
   (cilantro) leaves
2 medium oranges (480g),
   peeled, thinly sliced
to serve: Greek-style yogurt and
   sea salt flakes

1 Place chicken, breast-side down, on a chopping board. Using poultry shears, cut down both sides of the backbone and discard. Open out the chicken, turn it over and press down on the breastbone with the heel of your hand to flatten.

2 Combine garlic, lemon juice, paprika, harissa and oil in a large shallow dish; add chicken and turn to coat. Cover dish. Refrigerate for at least 2 hours or overnight.

3 Preheat a 7-litre air fryer to 180°C/350°F for 5 minutes.

4 Spray the air-fryer basket with oil. Taking care, place chicken, skin-side up, in the basket, then cover loosely with foil; at 180°C/350°F, cook for 20 minutes.

5 Remove foil; cook chicken for a further 20 minutes until juices run clear when a skewer is inserted into the thickest part of a thigh. Transfer to a large dish; cover with foil and allow to rest for 10 minutes.

6 Meanwhile, combine couscous and the boiling water in a large heatproof bowl; cover and allow to stand for 5 minutes or until liquid is absorbed. Fluff couscous with a fork. Stir in coriander and season to taste.

7 Serve chicken with couscous, oranges and yogurt, drizzled with any cooking juices from the bottom of the air-fryer pan. Sprinkle with sea salt flakes.

TIP Harissa brands can vary in heat, so use according to taste.

prep + cook time 1 hour (+ refrigeration & standing) serves 4

TESTING MEAT

Insert a meat thermometer into the thickest part of the beef. The internal temperature should reach:

rare 55–60°C/130–140°F

medium-rare 60–65°C/140–150°F

medium 65–70°C/150–160°F

medium—well done 70–75°C/160–170°F

well-done 75°C/170°F

HERB-CRUSTED ROAST BEEF
WITH CREAMY MUSHROOMS

---

1 boneless beef roasting joint such as top rump or sirloin, about 1.2kg (2½lb)
1 tbsp olive oil
⅔ cup (80g) panko breadcrumbs
¼ cup (20g) finely grated Parmesan
2 tbsp chopped flat-leaf parsley
1 tbsp chopped tarragon
¼ cup chopped chives
3 garlic cloves, crushed
¼ cup (70g) wholegrain mustard
1 tsp smoked paprika
olive oil cooking spray
150g (4½oz) chestnut (cremini) mushrooms, halved (or quartered if large)
150g (4½oz) button mushrooms, halved (or quartered if large)
¾ cup (180ml) double (heavy) cream
to serve: roast potatoes

1 Preheat a 7-litre air fryer to 200°C/400°F for 5 minutes.

2 Brush beef with 2 teaspoons of the oil and season.

3 Taking care, place beef in the air-fryer basket; at 200°C/400°F, cook for 15 minutes, turning halfway through cooking time, until browned all over.

4 Meanwhile, combine the breadcrumbs, Parmesan, parsley, tarragon, half of the chives and half of the garlic in a bowl; season. Transfer beef to a plate and pat dry with kitchen paper. Working quickly, spread 2 tablespoons of the mustard over the top and sides of beef, sprinkle with paprika, then firmly press on breadcrumb mixture. Generously spray breadcrumbs with oil.

5 Return beef to the air-fryer basket. Cover basket tightly with foil. Reset the temperature to 180°C/350°F; cook for 30 minutes. Remove foil.

6 Toss mushrooms in remaining oil and add to the air-fryer basket; at 180°C/350°F, cook, without foil, for a further 10 minutes until beef is medium or cooked to your liking (see Testing Meat to left) and mushrooms are browned. Transfer beef to a dish; cover loosely with foil and rest for 15 minutes.

7 Meanwhile, to make creamy mushrooms, combine cream and remaining garlic and mustard in a medium saucepan over a medium heat. Add the mushrooms and any cooking juices from the bottom of the air-fryer pan; bring to the boil. Reduce heat; simmer, stirring occasionally, for 5 minutes or until sauce slightly thickens. Stir in remaining chives and season to taste.

8 Thinly slice beef and serve with creamy mushrooms and roast potatoes.

MATCH IT Roast Potatoes 4 Ways, page 145.

prep + cook time 1 hour 20 minutes serves 6

TIKKA LAMB CUTLETS
WITH CARROT KOSHIMBIR

⅓ cup (80g) bottled tikka
  masala spice paste
1 tbsp lemon juice
½ cup (140g) Greek-style yogurt
12 French-trimmed lamb
  cutlets (600g)
olive oil cooking spray
to serve: steamed basmati rice
  and warm naan bread

CARROT KOSHIMBIR
2 medium carrots (240g),
  coarsely grated
½ cup (25g) shredded coconut
¼ cup (10g) firmly packed coriander
  (cilantro) leaves
1 long green chilli, thinly sliced
2 tbsp lemon juice

1 Combine spice paste, lemon juice and half of the yogurt in a large bowl; add lamb and toss to coat. Refrigerate for 1 hour.
2 Preheat a 7-litre air fryer to 200°C/400°F for 3 minutes.
3 To make carrot koshimbir, place carrot, coconut, half of the coriander, the chilli and lemon juice in a bowl; mix well. Season.
4 Taking care, line the air-fryer basket with a silicone mat, if available (see page 11). Spray lamb generously on both sides with oil and place in the basket; at 200°C/400°F, cook for 8 minutes, turning halfway through cooking time, for medium or until cooked to your liking.

5 Meanwhile, finely chop remaining coriander (from carrot koshimbir) and stir into remaining yogurt.
6 Serve lamb cutlets with steamed rice, warm naan bread, carrot koshimbir and coriander yogurt.

**prep + cook time
20 minutes
(+ refrigeration)
serves 4**

GREEK-
STYLE
POTATOES

MUSTARD & MINT
POTATOES

4 WAYS

PERI-PERI
POTATOES

FETA,
DILL &
BACON
POTATOES

GREEK-STYLE POTATOES

Preheat a 7-litre air fryer to 200°C/400°F for 3 minutes. Cut 1kg (2lb) baby potatoes into quarters lengthways. Place in a large bowl with 2 tbsp olive oil, 2 tsp dried oregano, 2 tbsp finely chopped rosemary and 4 crushed garlic cloves, then season; mix well to coat. Taking care, place potatoes in the air-fryer basket; at 200°C/400°F, cook for 20 minutes, turning halfway through cooking time, until golden and tender. Serve drizzled with 2 tbsp lemon juice.

MUSTARD & MINT POTATOES

Preheat a 7-litre air fryer to 200°C/400°F for 3 minutes. Cut 1kg (2lb) unpeeled baby potatoes in half lengthways. Place in a large bowl with 2 tbsp olive oil, then season; mix well to coat. Taking care, place potatoes in the air-fryer basket; at 200°C/400°F, cook for 20 minutes, turning halfway through cooking time, until golden and tender. Meanwhile, combine 1 tsp each of Dijon mustard and wholegrain mustard, 2 tbsp finely chopped mint, 1 tbsp olive oil and 3 tsp white wine vinegar in a large bowl; add potatoes and toss to coat. Serve scattered with mint leaves.

prep + cook time 30 minutes serves 6

ROAST POTATOES

PERI-PERI POTATOES

Preheat a 7-litre air fryer to 200°C/400°F for 3 minutes. Cut 1kg (2lb) baby potatoes in half widthways. Place in a large bowl with 2 tbsp olive oil, a 25g (¾oz) sachet of medium peri-peri seasoning and 3 crushed garlic cloves, then season; mix well to coat. Taking care, place potatoes in the air-fryer basket; at 200°C/400°F, cook for 20 minutes, turning halfway through cooking time, until golden and tender. Drizzle with peri-peri sauce for extra heat, if you like.

FETA, DILL & BACON POTATOES

Preheat a 7-litre air fryer to 200°C/400°F for 3 minutes. Cut 1kg (2lb) baby potatoes into quarters. Place in a large bowl with 2 tbsp olive oil, then season; mix well to coat. Taking care, place potatoes in the air-fryer basket; at 200°C/400°F, cook for 20 minutes, turning halfway through cooking time, until golden and tender. Add 150g (4½oz) chopped rindless back bacon rashers to the air-fryer basket for the last 7 minutes of cooking time. Meanwhile, combine 30g (1oz) crumbled feta, 1 tbsp chopped dill, 2 tbsp whole-egg mayonnaise and ¼ cup (65g) soured cream in a large bowl; add potatoes and toss to coat. Top with the crispy bacon and extra dill sprigs.

AUBERGINE PARMIGIANA "MEATBALL" SUBS

1 medium aubergine (eggplant)
(400g), peeled, cut into 4cm
(1½in) pieces
olive oil cooking spray
400g (12½oz) can chickpeas,
drained, rinsed
1 small red onion (100g),
finely chopped
2 garlic cloves, crushed
1 tbsp finely chopped
rosemary leaves
1¾ cups (140g) finely grated
Parmesan
1½ cups (150g) packaged
breadcrumbs
6 long soft bread rolls (300g)
1 cup (260g) tomato pasta
sauce, heated
40g (1½oz) baby rocket
(arugula) leaves
2 tsp balsamic vinegar

1 Preheat a 5.3-litre
air fryer to 200°C/400°F
for 3 minutes. Line a
baking tray with baking
parchment.
2 Taking care, place
aubergine in the air-fryer
basket and spray with oil;
at 200°C/400°F, cook
for 15 minutes until golden
and tender.
3 Transfer aubergine to
a food processor with
chickpeas, onion, garlic,
rosemary and 1 cup (80g)
of the Parmesan; process
until combined. Season.
Add 1 cup (100g) of the
breadcrumbs; pulse until
combined. Roll level
tablespoons of aubergine
mixture into 24 balls, then
coat in remaining
breadcrumbs; spray
generously with oil.

4 Place aubergine balls in
the basket; at 200°C/400°F,
cook for 20 minutes,
turning halfway through
cooking time, or until
golden and heated through.
5 Split rolls lengthways
along the top without
cutting all the way through;
spread sides with pasta
sauce. Fill each roll with
four eggplant "meatballs".
Place rolls in the basket;
at 200°C/400°F, cook for
5 minutes.
6 Meanwhile, combine
rocket and vinegar in
a small bowl.
7 To serve, sprinkle
remaining Parmesan over
"meatball" subs and top
with the rocket salad.

**prep + cook time 1 hour
serves 6**

LEMON & HERB PORK SCHNITZELS

½ cup (75g) plain (all-purpose) flour
2 eggs
⅓ cup (80ml) milk
2 garlic cloves, crushed
2 cups (150g) fresh breadcrumbs
   made from day-old bread
⅓ cup (25g) finely grated Parmesan
¼ cup chopped chives
1 tbsp finely chopped lemon thyme
2 tsp finely grated lemon zest
500g (1lb) thin pork leg escalopes
olive oil cooking spray
to serve: extra lemon thyme, sea
   salt flakes, aïoli, chips (see pages
   116–117 or use frozen) and
   lemon wedges

1 Place flour in a shallow bowl. Lightly beat eggs, milk and garlic in a second shallow bowl. Combine breadcrumbs, Parmesan, chives, thyme and lemon zest in a third shallow bowl. Dust pork in flour, shaking off excess, dip in egg mixture, then coat in breadcrumb mixture. Place schnitzels on a plate. Refrigerate for 30 minutes.
2 Preheat a 7-litre air fryer to 180°C/350°F for 3 minutes.
3 Spray schnitzels generously on both sides with oil. Taking care, place half of the schnitzels in the air-fryer basket; at 180°C/350°F, cook for 10 minutes, turning halfway through cooking time, until golden and cooked through. Transfer to a plate; cover loosely with foil to keep warm. Repeat cooking with remaining schnitzels.
4 Sprinkle schnitzels with extra thyme and sea salt flakes. Serve with aïoli, chips and lemon wedges.

MATCH IT Kale, Pear, Smoked Cheddar & Almond Salad, page 98.

prep + cook time
40 minutes
(+ refrigeration)
serves 4

RIDICULOUSLY
GOOD RIBS

2kg (4lb) American-style
    pork rib racks
olive oil cooking spray
1 cup (280g) barbecue sauce
3 cups (220g) shredded red cabbage
2 cups (180g) julienned carrot
1 medium green apple (150g),
    unpeeled, cored and thinly sliced
½ cup (125ml) coleslaw dressing
2 spring onions (scallions), green
    part only, very thinly sliced
    lengthways (see tip)

MARINADE
⅓ cup (80ml) apple cider vinegar
2 tbsp Worcestershire sauce
2 tbsp honey
2 garlic cloves, crushed
1 tbsp extra virgin olive oil

DRY SPICE RUB
1 tbsp smoked paprika
¼ tsp chilli powder
1 tsp chilli flakes
1½ tsp onion powder
1½ tsp garlic powder
2 tbsp light soft brown sugar

1 Using a small, sharp knife, remove the layer of membrane from the back of the rib racks (or ask your butcher to do this for you). Place rib racks in a large saucepan; cover well with water. Bring to the boil over a medium heat. Reduce heat to a simmer; cook for 45 minutes or until ribs are almost tender.

2 Meanwhile, combine marinade ingredients in a large bowl and dry spice rub ingredients in a small bowl. Drain ribs; add to marinade and turn to coat. Remove from marinade and sprinkle with dry spice rub. Using your hands, rub spices all over ribs; spray with oil.

3 Preheat a 5.3-litre air fryer to 180°C/350°F for 3 minutes.

4 Taking care, arrange rib racks in the air-fryer basket, standing them up and leaning them against the side of the basket and one another.

Reset the temperature to 160°C/325°F; cook for 20 minutes.

5 Brush ribs with three-quarters of the barbecue sauce; at 160°C/325°F, cook for 10 minutes until tender and glazed.

6 Meanwhile, combine cabbage, carrot, apple and dressing in a medium bowl. Top with spring onions.

7 Cut ribs into serving-sized pieces and brush with remaining barbecue sauce. Serve with coleslaw.

PREP IT You can prepare the ribs to the end of step 2 a day ahead; refrigerate until needed. As the ribs will be chilled, you may need to add an extra 5 minutes to the cooking time.
TIP To make spring onion curls, put in a small bowl of iced water for 5–7 minutes. Drain before using.

**prep + cook time
1½ hours serves 4**

151

SWEETCORN & SWEET POTATO HASH BROWNS
WITH SAUSAGES

750g (1½lb) chopped orange
  sweet potato
cooking oil spray
2 trimmed sweetcorn cobs (500g)
2 spring onions (scallions),
  finely chopped
4 breakfast-style pork
  sausages (500g)
½ cup (90g) rice flour
2 eggs
1¾ cups (135g) shredded coconut
to serve: baby spinach leaves
  and tomato chutney

1 Place sweet potato in the basket of a 5.3-litre air fryer and spray with oil; at 180°C/350°F, cook for 20 minutes, turning halfway through cooking time.
2 Taking care, add sweetcorn to the basket; at 180°C/350°F, cook for 5 minutes.
3 Transfer sweet potato to a bowl and mash. Using a sharp knife, cut kernels from sweetcorn cobs. Add kernels to mash with spring onion, then season; mix well.
4 Place sausages in the basket; at 180°C/350°F, cook for 15 minutes until browned and cooked through.
5 Meanwhile, shape heaped ⅓ cups of sweet potato mixture into patties; place on a tray lined with baking parchment. Place rice flour in a bowl. Lightly beat eggs in a shallow bowl. Place shredded coconut in a third bowl. Dust patties in flour, shaking off excess, dip in egg, then coat in coconut. Return to lined tray. Freeze for 10 minutes to set coating. (If not cooking immediately, refrigerate.)
6 Transfer sausages to a plate; cover to keep warm. Spray patties with oil on both sides and place in the basket. Reset the temperature to 160°C/325°F; cook for 10 minutes, turning halfway through cooking time, or until golden brown.
7 Serve sausages with hash browns, baby spinach leaves and tomato chutney.

TIP If you would like to ensure this recipe is gluten-free, buy gluten-free sausages and tomato chutney.

prep + cook time
1¼ hours (+ refrigeration)
serves 4

CHEESY BACON PULL-APART

**prep + cook time 30 minutes
(+ standing) serves 8**

Divide 1 quantity Basic Dough (see recipe opposite)
into eight equal portions; roll each portion into
a ball. Arrange dough balls, 2cm (¾in) apart, in a
greased 23cm (9¼in) round cake tin; cover with
cling film. Allow to stand in a warm place for
20 minutes or until doubled in size. Preheat a
7-litre air fryer to 200°C/400°F for 5 minutes.
Taking care, place pan in the air-fryer basket.
Reset the temperature to 170°C/340°F; cook for
15 minutes. Brush bread with 25g (¾oz) melted
butter, then sprinkle with ¾ cup (50g) grated
Cheddar and 4 finely chopped centre-cut (back)
bacon rashers; cook for 8 minutes until bread
is golden and cooked through.

GARLIC & PARMESAN TWIST

prep + cook time 40 minutes (+ standing) serves 6

Combine 1 tbsp olive oil, 25g (¾oz) melted butter,
3 crushed garlic cloves and 2 tbsp finely chopped
chives. Divide 1 quantity Basic Dough (see recipe
opposite) into three portions; roll each portion into
a 30cm (12in) rope shape. Place ropes, side by side,
on a 25cm (10in) square piece of baking parchment;
pinch at one end to join. Brush with three-quarters
of the butter mixture, then sprinkle with 2 tbsp finely
grated Parmesan. Plait ropes loosely, then pinch end
tightly to join; cover with a clean tea towel. Allow
to stand in a warm place for 20 minutes or until
doubled in size. Preheat a 7-litre air fryer to
200°C/400°F for 5 minutes. Taking care, use the
baking parchment as an aid to lower the dough
plait diagonally into the air-fryer basket. Brush
with half of the remaining butter mixture. Reset
the temperature to 170°C/340°F; cook for 18
minutes. Brush with remaining butter mixture,
then sprinkle with 2 tbsp finely grated Parmesan;
cook for 5 minutes until bread is golden and
cooked through.

TOMATO PESTO FOCACCIA

prep + cook time 40 minutes (+ standing) serves 6

Preheat a 7-litre air fryer to 200°C/400°F for
5 minutes. Roll 1 quantity Basic Dough (see recipe
opposite) into a 23cm (9¼in) round; place on a
large piece of baking parchment. Using fingertips,
press dimples all over the dough. Trim baking
parchment so that it is 2cm (¾in) larger all
around than the dough base. Taking care, use
the parchment as an aid to lower the focaccia
into the air-fryer basket. Reset the temperature
to 170°C/340°F; cook for 15 minutes. Combine
1 tbsp olive oil and 2 tbsp sun-dried tomato
pesto in a small bowl. Spread pesto mixture over
focaccia, then sprinkle with 2 sliced garlic cloves
and 1 tsp sea salt flakes; cook for 7 minutes until
focaccia is golden and cooked through. Top with
basil leaves to serve.

MIXED-SEED BUNS

prep + cook time 30 minutes (+ standing) serves 8

Combine ¼ cup pumpkin and sunflower seed mix,
2 tbsp pine nuts, 1 tbsp linseeds (flaxseeds) and
1 tbsp sesame seeds. Knead half of the seed
mixture into 1 quantity Basic Dough (see recipe
opposite). Divide dough into eight portions; roll
each portion into a ball. Place on a tray lined with
baking parchment; cover with a clean tea towel.
Allow to stand in a warm place for 20 minutes or
until doubled in size. Preheat a 7-litre air fryer to
200°C/400°F for 5 minutes. Taking care, line the
air-fryer basket with baking parchment. Place the
dough balls, 2cm (¾in) apart, in the basket. Cut
three shallow slits on the top of each dough ball.
Lightly brush tops with 1 lightly beaten egg, then
sprinkle with remaining seed mixture. Reset the
temperature to 170°C/340°F; cook for 15 minutes
until buns are golden and cooked through.

BASIC DOUGH

Combine 600g (1¼lb) packet white bread mix and 2 tsp yeast in a large bowl. Add 1⅓ cups (330ml) lukewarm water; mix to form a dough. Knead dough on a lightly floured surface for 10 minutes (or 6 minutes in an electric mixer fitted with a dough hook) or until dough is smooth and elastic. Return dough to cleaned bowl; cover with cling film. Allow to stand in a warm place for 30 minutes or until doubled in size. Using your fist, punch down dough to remove air. Knead on a lightly floured surface for 2 minutes or until smooth. Continue with one of the recipe variations to the left.

4 WAYS

BREAD

CHEESY BACON PULL-APART

TOMATO PESTO FOCACCIA

GARLIC & PARMESAN TWIST

MIXED-SEED BUNS

JAPANESE SALMON

WITH MISO SAUCE

2 tbsp mirin
2 tbsp cooking sake
2 tbsp soy sauce
800g (1½lb) centre-cut piece
    skinless boneless salmon
8 spring onions (scallions), trimmed
2 tsp sesame seeds, toasted

MISO SAUCE
2 tbsp white (shiro) miso
2 tbsp rice wine vinegar
1½ tbsp honey
1½ tbsp soy sauce

1 To make yakitori marinade, combine mirin, sake and soy sauce in a small bowl.

2 To make miso sauce, blend ingredients in a small blender until smooth.

3 Preheat a 5.3-litre air fryer to 160°C/325°F for 3 minutes.

4 Cut salmon into 2cm (¾in) pieces; thread onto six metal or bamboo skewers. Brush all over with the marinade.

5 Taking care, line the air-fryer basket with baking parchment. Place spring onions in the basket; at 160°C/325°F, cook for 5 minutes until tender. Transfer to a platter; cover to keep warm.

6 Place half of the skewers in the basket; at 160°C/325°F, cook for 5 minutes or until cooked to your liking. Transfer to platter; cover to keep warm. Repeat cooking with remaining skewers.

7 Serve the salmon and spring onions drizzled with miso sauce; sprinkle with sesame seeds.

SERVE IT Serve with microwaveable brown rice and quinoa, and lime cheeks.

**prep + cook time
35 minutes makes 6**

SWAP IT The yakitori marinade and miso sauce also work well with large prawns (shrimp). If using prawns, cook them for 5 minutes.

HOISIN PORK
WITH PEANUT RICE

⅓ cup (190g) hoisin sauce

⅓ cup (80ml) salt-reduced soy sauce

2 tbsp Shaohsing rice wine

2 tbsp honey

¼ cup (55g) firmly packed
   light soft brown sugar

4 garlic cloves, crushed

½ tsp Chinese five-spice powder

4 x 150g (4½oz) pork
   shoulder steaks

450g (14½oz) packet microwaveable
   jasmine rice

½ cup (70g) unsalted roasted
   peanuts, coarsely chopped

2 spring onions (scallions),
   thinly sliced

4 baby cucumbers (240g),
   thinly sliced lengthways

to serve: extra hoisin sauce

1 Combine hoisin sauce, soy sauce, rice wine, honey, sugar, garlic and five-spice powder in a large shallow dish; add pork and turn to coat. Cover dish. Refrigerate for at least 2 hours or overnight.

2 Line the bottom of a 7-litre air-fryer pan with foil. Preheat air fryer to 180°C/350°F for 3 minutes.

3 Taking care, place pork in the air-fryer basket, reserving the marinade; at 180°C/350°F, cook for 15 minutes, turning and basting pork with reserved marinade halfway through cooking time.

4 Reset the temperature to 200°C/400°F; cook pork for a further 5 minutes, basting with reserved marinade, or until charred and cooked through. Transfer to a dish; cover with foil and allow to rest for 5 minutes.

5 Meanwhile, heat rice according to packet directions. Transfer to a medium heatproof bowl; stir in peanuts and half of the spring onion.

6 Slice pork; serve with rice, cucumber and remaining spring onion. Drizzle pork with any cooking juices from the bottom of the air-fryer pan and extra hoisin sauce.

**prep + cook time
35 minutes
(+ refrigeration)
serves 4**

STUFFED LEG OF LAMB
WITH APRICOT & PISTACHIO

½ cup (80g) finely chopped
    dried apricots
¼ cup (60ml) orange juice
30g (1oz) butter, chopped
1 medium onion (150g),
    finely chopped
1 cup (100g) coarse fresh
    sourdough breadcrumbs
    (made from day-old bread)
¼ cup (30g) pistachios, roasted,
    finely chopped
2 tbsp finely chopped sage
1.2kg (2½lb) boneless leg of lamb
1 tbsp olive oil
1 garlic bulb, halved
1 cup (250ml) gravy, warmed
to serve: roast potatoes (see tip)
    and broccolini (Tenderstem
    broccoli)

1 Combine the apricots and orange juice in a bowl; set aside for 20 minutes.
2 Meanwhile, melt butter in a medium frying pan over a medium heat; add onion and cook, stirring, for 5 minutes or until soft. Stir in breadcrumbs; cook for 1 minute or until breadcrumbs are golden. Remove from heat; stir in pistachios, sage and apricot mixture.
3 Preheat a 7-litre air fryer to 200°C/400°F for 5 minutes.
4 Untie and unroll lamb; place, skin-side down, on a chopping board. Using a sharp knife, cut three 1cm (½in) deep slits along the length of the lamb to open up the flesh. Press pistachio mixture along the centre of the lamb; roll up to enclose filling. Tie lamb at 2.5cm (1in) intervals with kitchen string to secure. Rub all over with oil and season.

5 Taking care, place lamb and garlic in the air-fryer basket. Reset the temperature to 170°C/325°F; cook for 25 minutes. Turn lamb over and cover with foil; cook for a further 25 minutes for medium or until cooked to your liking.
6 Transfer lamb and garlic to a dish; cover loosely with foil and allow to rest for 10 minutes.
7 Serve slices of lamb with garlic, warm gravy, roast potatoes and broccolini.

TIP To roast potatoes, cook 1kg (2lb) halved fingerling potatoes tossed in olive oil at 200°C/400°F for 20 minutes, turning halfway through cooking time, until golden and tender. Season with sea salt flakes to serve.

**prep + cook time
1 hour 15 minutes
serves 6**

TIP While traditionally eaten at breakfast, this Maghrebi dish can also be enjoyed as a light supper.

WHITE BEAN
SHAKSHUKA

---

2 tbsp finely chopped coriander
  (cilantro) stems
2 spring onions (scallions),
  finely chopped
½ tsp ground cumin
½ tsp smoked paprika
2 tsp extra virgin olive oil
400g (12½oz) jar arrabbiata
  pasta sauce
400g (12½oz) can cannellini beans,
  drained, rinsed
1 chargrilled red pepper (60g), sliced
4 eggs, at room temperature
1 medium avocado (250g), diced
to serve: purple salad leaves and
  chargrilled split pitta bread

1 Oil a 3-cup (750ml) 20cm (8in) ovenproof dish; ensure the dish will fit into a 5.3-litre air fryer. (You can also use two large ramekins.)
2 Put coriander stems, spring onions, spices and oil in the dish, then place in the air-fryer basket; at 180°C/350°F, cook for 3 minutes until fragrant.
3 Taking care, add pasta sauce, beans and pepper to dish; stir until combined. Cover top of dish with foil; at 180°C/350°F, cook for a further 10 minutes until mixture is hot.
4 Make four indents in the bean mixture and break an egg into each, then season with salt and freshly ground black pepper; at 180°C/350°F, cook for 8 minutes until eggs are just set or cooked to your liking.
5 Top shakshuka with avocado and salad leaves. Serve with chargrilled pitta bread.

prep + cook time
25 minutes serves 2

CRACKING PORK BELLY
& ASIAN SALAD

1kg (2lb) piece boneless pork belly, rind scored (see tips)
1 tbsp salt flakes
½ tsp Chinese five-spice powder
olive oil cooking spray
1 Lebanese cucumber (130g), thinly sliced lengthways
1 small red onion (100g), thinly sliced
¼ medium Chinese leaf (napa cabbage) (250g), shredded
1 cup (30g) Thai basil leaves
1 cup (30g) coriander (cilantro) leaves
2 cups (60g) baby spinach
2 long red chillies, deseeded, thinly sliced
1 spring onion (scallion), thinly sliced
1 lime (65g), cut into wedges

GINGER DRESSING
1 lemongrass stalk, finely chopped
1 tbsp finely grated fresh root ginger
1½ tbsp soy sauce
1½ tbsp lime juice
1 tbsp sesame oil
1 tbsp rice wine vinegar
1 tbsp caster (superfine) sugar

1 Preheat a 5.3-litre air fryer to 180°C/350°F for 3 minutes.
2 Pat pork dry with kitchen paper. Combine half of the sea salt flakes and the five-spice powder; rub into pork rind.
3 Taking care, place pork in the air-fryer basket and spray with oil. Reset temperature to 200°C/400°F; cook for 25 minutes until pork rind crackles.
4 Reset the temperature to 160°C/325°F; cook for a further 30 minutes until pork is tender, or an internal temperature of 70–75°C/160–170°F is reached on a meat thermometer. (Cover pork with foil if overbrowning.)
5 Meanwhile, to make ginger dressing, whisk ingredients in a small bowl.

6 Layer cucumber, red onion, Chinese leaf, herbs, spinach and chilli on a platter.
7 Thickly slice pork and place on top of salad. Scatter with spring onion and sprinkle with remaining sea salt flakes; drizzle with the dressing. Serve with lime wedges.

TIPS A Stanley knife or similar is the best tool for scoring the pork rind; alternatively, you can ask your butcher to do it for you. As soon as you get home, place the pork on a tray, uncovered, in the fridge for up to 2 days, to dry out the rind – this will help with crackling the rind.

prep + cook time
1¼ hours serves 4

GREEN CURRY CHICKEN
WITH PICKLED RADISH

2 tbsp Thai green curry paste
1 tbsp extra virgin olive oil
1 tbsp fish sauce
1 tbsp lime juice
1 tbsp light soft brown sugar
4 chicken thighs (800g), skin on
to serve: microwaveable coconut
    rice and finely chopped spring
    onion (scallion)

PICKLED RADISH
¼ cup (60ml) rice wine vinegar
1 tsp light soft brown sugar
½ tsp sea salt flakes
6 mixed radishes (220g), trimmed,
    thinly sliced (see tip)

1 To make pickled radish, combine vinegar, sugar and salt flakes in a small bowl; add ¼ cup (60ml) cold water and stir to combine. Add radishes; mix through to combine. Set aside until needed.
2 Preheat a 7-litre air fryer to 180°C/350°F for 3 minutes.
3 Combine curry paste, oil, fish sauce, lime juice and sugar in a large bowl; add chicken and turn to coat.
4 Taking care, place chicken, skin-side down, in the air-fryer basket; at 180°C/350°F, cook for 20 minutes, turning after 8 minutes, or until golden and cooked through. (There will be a little bit of smoke in the initial 5–7 minutes of cooking; however, this will stop with further cooking.)
5 Serve chicken on coconut rice, topped with chopped spring onion and drained pickled radish.

TIP We used a mixture of red and watermelon radishes for the pickle.

prep + cook time
35 minutes serves 4

CHICKEN PARMIGIANA

3 skinless boneless chicken
   breasts (600g)
½ cup (75g) plain (all-purpose) flour
2 eggs
1 garlic clove, crushed
1½ cups (110g) panko breadcrumbs
1 tsp sweet paprika
2 tsp finely grated lemon zest
1 tbsp finely chopped
   flat-leaf parsley
cooking oil spray
1 cup (280g) tomato pasta sauce
160g (5oz) mozzarella, sliced
¼ cup (20g) finely grated Parmesan
to serve: baby rocket (arugula),
   roasted vine tomatoes (see tip)
   and lemon wedges

1 Cut chicken fillets in half horizontally to make six pieces. Place chicken between two sheets of cling film; pound gently with a rolling pin until even in thickness.

2 Place flour in a small bowl and season. Lightly beat eggs, garlic and 1 tablespoon water in a second bowl. Place breadcrumbs, paprika, lemon zest and parsley in a third bowl. Dust chicken in flour, shaking off excess, dip in egg, then coat in breadcrumb mixture. Spray chicken escalopes generously on both sides with oil.

3 Preheat a 5.3-litre air fryer to 180°C/350°F for 3 minutes.

4 Taking care, place three escalopes in the air-fryer basket; at 180°C/350°F, cook for 12 minutes until golden brown and cooked through. Transfer to a tray; cover to keep warm. Repeat cooking with remaining escalopes.

5 Return three escalopes to the basket. Top each with 2 tablespoons pasta sauce; scatter with half of the mozzarella and Parmesan; at 180°C/350°F, cook for 8 minutes until cheeses are melted and bubbling. Repeat with remaining escalopes, pasta sauce, mozzarella and Parmesan.

6 Serve chicken with baby rocket, roasted tomatoes and lemon wedges.

**prep + cook time 1 hour
makes 6**

TIP To roast vine tomatoes, add them to the edge of the basket with the escalopes in step 5; cook for 6 minutes.

CHEAT'S SAUSAGE CASSOULET

500g (1lb) thick pork sausages
olive oil cooking spray
1 tbsp extra virgin olive oil
1 medium onion (150g),
    finely chopped
2 bacon rashers (160g), thinly sliced
2 garlic cloves, crushed
1 medium red pepper (200g),
    coarsely chopped
1 medium courgette (zucchini)
    (120g), coarsely chopped
250g (8oz) baby plum tomatoes
½ cup (125ml) dry red wine
1½ cups (390g) tomato pasta sauce
3 sprigs of thyme
400g (12½oz) can butterbeans
    (lima beans), drained, rinsed
1½ cups (105g) coarse fresh
    sourdough breadcrumbs
    (made from day-old bread)
⅓ cup (25g) grated Gruyère cheese
⅓ cup (20g) chopped
    flat-leaf parsley
to serve: sea salt flakes

1 Preheat a 7-litre air fryer to 200°C/400°F for 3 minutes.

2 Spray sausages with oil. Taking care, place sausages in the air-fryer basket; at 200°C/400°F, cook for 8 minutes, turning halfway through cooking time, or until browned.

3 Meanwhile, heat oil in a large frying pan over a medium-high heat; cook onion and bacon, stirring, for 5 minutes or until onion is softened and bacon is crisp. Add garlic, pepper and courgette; cook, stirring, for 4 minutes or until vegetables are lightly browned. Add tomatoes and wine; bring to the boil. Add pasta sauce and thyme; return to the boil.

4 Transfer sausages to a board and coarsely chop; add to tomato mixture with butterbeans. Transfer mixture to a deep 20cm (8in) round ovenproof dish.

5 Taking care, wipe the air-fryer basket clean; place the ovenproof dish in the basket. Reset the temperature to 180°C/350°F; cook for 8 minutes.

6 Meanwhile, combine breadcrumbs, Gruyère and parsley in a bowl.

7 Top cassoulet with breadcrumb mixture, spray with oil, then press crumbs down firmly; at 180°C/350°F, cook for 5 minutes until breadcrumbs are golden.

8 Sprinkle cassoulet with sea salt flakes to serve.

**prep + cook time
40 minutes serves 4**

SOUTHERN FRIED CHICKEN

1 whole chicken, about 1.6kg (3¼lb)
  (see tip)
1 cup (250ml) buttermilk
1 egg, lightly beaten
1¼ cups (185g) plain (all-
  purpose) flour
2 tsp smoked paprika
1 tsp garlic powder
1 tsp onion flakes
1 tsp dried oregano
1 tsp sea salt flakes
1 tsp ground cumin
½ tsp chilli powder
olive oil cooking spray
to serve: extra sea salt flakes,
  mayonnaise and hot sauce

1 Using a sharp knife, cut chicken into eight pieces. Make two deep slits through the thickest part of the meat to the bone in each chicken piece.
2 Combine buttermilk and egg in a large bowl, then season; add chicken and turn to coat. Cover bowl. Refrigerate for 6 hours or overnight.
3 Combine flour, paprika, garlic powder, onion flakes, oregano, salt, cumin and chilli powder in a large bowl; season.
4 Working with one piece of chicken at a time, drain excess buttermilk mixture, then roll chicken in flour mixture to coat. Repeat with remaining chicken and flour mixture; spray generously all over with oil.
5 Preheat a 7-litre air fryer to 200°C/400°F for 3 minutes.

6 Taking care, line the air-fryer basket with a silicone mat, if available (see page 11). Place chicken in the basket; at 200°C/400°F, cook for 10 minutes.
7 Turn chicken over. Reset the temperature to 180°C/350°F; cook for 10 minutes or until crisp and cooked through. (The breast pieces may cook a little quicker than the thighs and legs.)
8 Sprinkle chicken with extra sea salt flakes. Serve with mayonnaise swirled with a little hot sauce.

**prep + cook time
40 minutes
(+ refrigeration)
serves 4**

TIP You could also use 1.6kg (3¼lb) chicken pieces on the bone; you may need to adjust the cooking time depending on the pieces.

AIR BAKE

The air fryer isn't just about savoury
food, it's also brilliant at sweet treats too.
Make all your favourite baked recipes,
such as cakes, puddings, muffins,
brownies, cookies, tarts, pies and more
– including a couple of savoury options.

CHOCOLATE CAKE
WITH FUDGE ICING

125g (4oz) butter, softened
1 tsp vanilla extract
¾ cup (165g) caster
   (superfine) sugar
2 eggs
1¼ cups (185g) self-raising flour
½ cup (50g) unsweetened
   cocoa powder
½ cup (125ml) milk

FUDGE ICING
50g (1¾oz) butter, chopped
⅓ cup (75g) firmly packed
   light soft brown sugar
1 tbsp milk
1 cup (160g) icing
   (confectioners') sugar
2 tbsp cocoa powder

1 Preheat a 7-litre air fryer to 160°C/325°F for 5 minutes. Grease a deep 20cm (8in) round cake tin; line bottom and side of tin with baking parchment.

2 Beat butter, vanilla, sugar, eggs, sifted flour and cocoa, and milk in a large bowl with an electric mixer on low speed until combined. Increase speed to medium; beat for 3 minutes or until mixture is smooth and paler in colour. Spoon mixture into cake tin. Cover tin with a piece of greased foil.

3 Taking care, place cake tin in the air-fryer basket; at 160°C/325°F, cook for 1 hour until a skewer inserted into the centre comes out clean. Remove from the basket. Leave cake in tin for 10 minutes before turning, top-side up, onto a wire rack to cool.

4 Meanwhile, to make fudge icing, stir butter, brown sugar and milk in a small saucepan over a low heat until sugar dissolves. Remove from heat. Sift icing sugar and cocoa powder into a small bowl; gradually whisk in hot butter mixture until smooth. Cover bowl. Refrigerate for 40 minutes or until icing thickens.

5 Beat icing with a wooden spoon until spreadable. Spread top of cooled cake with fudge icing.

prep + cook time
1¼ hours
(+ refrigeration)
serves 12

TIP Make sure that you are wearing a long-sleeved top while piping the churros mixture into the hot air-fryer basket, as this will protect you from touching the hot sides.

CHURROS
WITH CHOCOLATE SAUCE

60g (2oz) butter
pinch of sea salt flakes
½ cup (125ml) cold water
⅓ cup (75g) caster (superfine) sugar
½ cup (75g) plain (all-purpose) flour
2 eggs, lightly beaten
olive oil cooking spray
1 tsp ground cinnamon
125g (4oz) dark (semi-sweet)
   chocolate, chopped
½ cup (125ml) double (heavy) cream

1 Bring butter, salt, the cold water and 1 tablespoon of the caster sugar to the boil in a medium saucepan. Add sifted flour; beat with a wooden spoon over a high heat until mixture comes away from the bottom and side of the pan to form a smooth ball. Transfer to a small bowl; beat in egg, in two batches, with a wooden spoon until mixture becomes glossy. Spoon into a piping bag fitted with a 2cm (¾in) fluted tube.

2 Preheat a 7-litre air fryer to 180°C/350°F for 3 minutes.

3 Spray the air-fryer basket with oil. Taking care, pipe four 10cm (4in) lengths of batter, 5cm (2in) apart, into the basket (see tip); at 180°C/350°F, cook for 12 minutes until golden and crisp. Repeat cooking with remaining batter to make a total of 8 churros.

4 Meanwhile, to make cinnamon sugar, combine cinnamon and remaining sugar in a shallow bowl. Immediately place hot churros in cinnamon sugar and toss to coat.

5 To make chocolate sauce, place chocolate and cream in a small saucepan over a low-medium heat; stir until smooth and combined.

6 Serve churros with warm chocolate sauce.

prep + cook time
45 minutes makes 8

LEMON CURD SCONES

2⅓ cups (375g) self-raising flour
⅓ tsp baking powder
pinch of fine salt
2 tbsp demerara (raw) sugar
300ml buttermilk
¼ cup (80g) ready-made lemon curd
olive oil cooking spray
to serve: fruit jam (choose
    your favourite flavour) and
    whipped or clotted cream

1 Sift flour, baking powder, salt and sugar into a large bowl. Make a well in the centre; pour in combined buttermilk and lemon curd. Using a flat-bladed knife, gently stir until dough just comes together.
2 Turn out dough onto a lightly floured work surface. Using your hands, briefly knead. Pat out until dough is 3cm (1¼in) thick.
3 Using a floured cutter, cut 5.5cm (2¼in) rounds from dough. Press scraps of dough together until 3cm (1¼in) thick. Repeat cutting to get a total of 9 scones. Brush top of scones with any buttermilk left in the carton or with 1 tablespoon milk.

4 Preheat a 7-litre air fryer to 180°C/350°F for 3 minutes.
5 Spray the air-fryer basket with oil. Taking care, place scones, side by side, in the basket. Reset the temperature to 160°C/325°F; cook for 17 minutes.
6 Serve warm scones with jam and cream.

SERVE IT You can also serve the scones with lemon curd and whipped cream, if you like.

prep + cook time
35 minutes makes 9

PEANUT BUTTER BROWNIES

125g (4oz) butter, chopped
200g (6½oz) dark chocolate
   (at least 45% cocoa solids),
   chopped
½ cup (110g) caster
   (superfine) sugar
½ cup (160g) ready-made
   caramel dessert filling
¼ cup (70g) crunchy peanut butter
2 eggs, lightly beaten
1 cup (150g) plain (all-purpose) flour
¼ cup (35g) self-raising flour
1 tbsp unsweetened cocoa powder

1 Stir butter and chocolate in a medium saucepan over a low heat until just smooth. Remove from heat; stir in sugar. Allow to cool for 10 minutes.

2 Preheat a 7-litre air fryer to 160°C/325°F for 5 minutes. Grease a 20cm (8in) square cake tin; line bottom and sides with baking parchment.

3 Microwave caramel filling for 30 seconds or until softened; stir in the peanut butter.

4 Stir egg into chocolate mixture, then sifted flours and cocoa. Spread half of the brownie mixture into cake tin; dollop with half of the peanut butter mixture. Gently spread remaining brownie mixture over the top, then dollop with remaining peanut butter mixture. Using a skewer, swirl the peanut butter mixture through the brownie mixture. Cover tin tightly with foil.

5 Taking care, place cake tin in the air-fryer basket; at 160°C/325°F, cook for 25 minutes.

6 Remove foil; cook for a further 10 minutes or until brownie is just set on top. Remove from the basket. Leave brownie to cool in tin.

7 Cut brownie into 12 pieces.

**prep + cook time
55 minutes makes 12**

CARAMELIZED ONION, DILL & CARAWAY SAUSAGE ROLLS

500g (1lb) pork mince (ground pork)
1 cup (100g) packaged breadcrumbs
1 egg, lightly beaten
2 garlic cloves, crushed
¼ cup finely chopped dill
1 tbsp caraway seeds, plus
  1 tsp extra
½ cup (150g) caramelized onion
  relish or chutney
2 tsp malt vinegar
3 sheets of frozen puff pastry,
  just thawed
2 egg yolks
cooking oil spray
to serve: brown sauce or
  barbecue sauce

1 Preheat a 5.3-litre air fryer to 180°C/350°F for 3 minutes.
2 Combine pork mince, breadcrumbs, egg, garlic, dill, the 1 tablespoon caraway seeds, relish and vinegar in a large bowl; season well.
3 Cut pastry sheets in half. Spoon or pipe pork mixture in a line through the centre of each pastry piece; roll pastry over to enclose filling. Cut each roll into four pieces; place, seam-side down, on a tray lined with baking parchment. Combine egg yolks and 1 teaspoon water in a small bowl. Brush pastry with egg and sprinkle with extra 1 teaspoon caraway seeds.

4 Spray the air-fryer basket with oil. Taking care, place 8 sausage rolls in the basket; at 180°C/350°F, cook for 15 minutes until puffed and cooked through. Transfer to a wire rack. Repeat cooking two more times with the remaining sausage rolls.
5 Serve hot sausage rolls with sauce.

PREP IT Sausage rolls can be prepared to the end of step 3 a day ahead; refrigerate until ready to bake.

KEEP IT Sausage rolls can be frozen in an airtight container for up to 3 months.

**prep + cook time
1 hour makes 24**

STRAWBERRY
POP TARTS

250g (8oz) strawberries,
   finely chopped
2 tbsp strawberry jam
1 tbsp cornflour (cornstarch)
4 sheets of frozen shortcrust pastry,
   just thawed
1 egg, lightly beaten
½ cup (80g) icing (confectioners')
   sugar
2 tsp cold water
pink food colouring, to tint
to decorate: 100s & 1000s
   (nonpareils) or other sugar
   sprinkles

1 Combine strawberries, jam and cornflour in a small bowl. Cut each pastry sheet into six 8cm x 10cm (3¼in x 4in) rectangles. Place a level tablespoon of strawberry mixture in the centre of half the pastry rectangles. Brush edges of pastry with a little egg. Cover filling with remaining pastry rectangles; using a fork, press edges together to seal.

2 Preheat a 7-litre air fryer to 180°C/350°F for 3 minutes.

3 Taking care, place half of the tarts in the air-fryer basket; at 180°C/350°F, cook for 12 minutes, turning after 10 minutes of cooking time, until pastry is golden and cooked.

Transfer to a wire rack to cool. Repeat cooking with remaining tarts.

4 Combine icing sugar, the 2 teaspoons cold water and food colouring in a small bowl. Spoon icing over cooled tarts; sprinkle immediately with 100s & 1000s. Allow to stand until icing sets.

**prep + cook time
35 minutes (+ standing)
makes 12**

BERRY FRANGIPANE GALETTE

1 cup (150g) plain (all-purpose) flour
2 tbsp caster (superfine) sugar
60g (2oz) chilled butter, chopped
1 egg yolk
2 tbsp ground almonds
150g (4½oz) frozen mixed berries
2 tsp cornflour (cornstarch)
to serve: icing (confectioners') sugar
    and ice cream

FRANGIPANE FILLING
60g (2oz) butter, softened
¼ cup (55g) caster (superfine) sugar
1 tsp vanilla extract
1 egg yolk
⅔ cup (80g) ground almonds
1½ tbsp plain (all-purpose) flour

1 To make pastry, process flour, sugar and butter in a food processor until mixture resembles fine breadcrumbs. Add egg yolk; process until dough just comes together. Turn out onto a work surface and shape into a disc; wrap in cling film. Refrigerate for 30 minutes.

2 Meanwhile, to make frangipane filling, beat butter, sugar and vanilla in a small bowl with an electric mixer until pale and creamy. Beat in egg yolk until combined. Stir in ground almonds and flour until combined.

3 Preheat a 7-litre air fryer to 180°C/350°F for 5 minutes.

4 Roll out pastry between two sheets of baking parchment until 3mm (⅛in) thick. Using a plate or cake tin, cut out a 25cm (10in) round from pastry; discard offcuts. Sprinkle ground almonds over pastry round, then evenly spread with frangipane, leaving a 3cm (1in) border. Toss berries in cornflour to coat, shaking off excess; scatter over frangipane. Fold pastry border up and over filling.

5 Taking care, and using the parchment as an aid, lower the galette into the air-fryer basket, then cover basket tightly with foil; at 180°C/350°F, cook for 30 minutes.

6 Remove foil. Reset the temperature to 160°C/325°F; cook for a further 15–18 minutes until pastry is golden and frangipane is cooked through. Taking care, and using the parchment as an aid, lift the galette from the basket.

7 Dust the galette with icing sugar and serve with ice cream.

prep + cook time
1 hour 10 minutes
(+ refrigeration)
serves 6

APPLEY PIE ROLLS

400g (12½oz) can fruit filling apple slices, chopped
¼ cup (40g) sultanas (golden raisins)
1½ tbsp caster (superfine) sugar
½ tsp ground cinnamon
1½ tbsp ground almonds
8 x 21.5cm (8¾in) frozen spring roll wrappers, thawed (see tip)
olive oil cooking spray
to serve: icing (confectioners') sugar, to dust, and vanilla ice cream

1 Combine apple, sultanas, sugar, cinnamon and ground almonds in a medium bowl.

2 Place a spring roll wrapper on a clean work surface. Place 2 level tablespoons of filling in a line a third up from the bottom edge, leaving a 4cm (1½in) border on each side. Fold bottom of wrapper over filling once, fold in the sides, then roll up to enclose filling; brush the join with a little water to seal. Repeat with remaining spring roll wrappers and filling to make 8 rolls in total.

3 Preheat a 7-litre air fryer to 200°C/400°F for 3 minutes.

4 Spray rolls generously all over with oil. Taking care, place rolls in the air-fryer basket; at 200°C/400°F, cook for 15 minutes until golden brown.

5 Dust rolls with icing sugar and serve with ice cream.

**prep + cook time
35 minutes makes 8**

TIP You can find spring roll wrappers in the freezer section of Asian grocers or supermarkets.

KEEP IT Cookies will
keep in an airtight
container for up to
2 weeks.

BASIC VANILLA BUTTER COOKIES

125g (4oz) butter, softened
½ cup (110g) caster (superfine)
  sugar, plus 2 tbsp extra
1 tsp vanilla extract
1 egg yolk
1½ cups (185g) plain
  (all-purpose) flour
to serve: icing (confectioners') sugar,
  to dust

1 Beat butter, the ½ cup (110g) caster sugar and vanilla in a small bowl with an electric mixer until light and fluffy. Beat in egg yolk until combined. Sift flour, in two batches, into butter mixture; mix well.
2 Knead dough on a lightly floured surface until smooth. Using your hands, shape dough into a 25cm (10in) long log. Place the extra 2 tablespoons caster sugar on a plate; roll log in the sugar. Wrap log in baking parchment. Freeze for 1 hour or until firm.
3 Remove log from the freezer. Allow to stand for 10 minutes. Slice into 15 rounds, each about 1.5cm (¾in) thick.
4 Preheat a 7-litre air fryer to 160°C/325°F for 5 minutes.

5 Taking care, line the air-fryer basket with baking parchment. Place half of the cookies, 2cm (¾in) apart, in the basket (place remaining cookies in the fridge until needed); at 160°C/350°F, cook for 12 minutes until golden. Remove the basket from the air-fryer pan. Leave cookies in the basket for 10 minutes before transferring to a wire rack to cool completely. Repeat cooking with remaining cookies.
6 Dust cookies with icing sugar.

**prep + cook time
40 minutes (+ freezing, standing & cooling)
makes 15**

193

TRIPLE-CHOC

Add ⅓ cup (80g) each of milk, dark and white chocolate chips to 1 quantity Basic Vanilla Butter Cookies recipe (page 193) just before adding the flour in step 1. Roll level tablespoons of mixture into balls. Flatten balls until 1cm (½in) thick. Freeze for 20 minutes. Bake as recipe directs in steps 4 and 5.

TIP You could also use 180g (5½oz) hand-chopped chocolate of a single type, if you like.

ORANGE & PECAN

Add 1 tsp finely grated orange zest and ½ cup (60g) chopped toasted pecans to 1 quantity Basic Vanilla Butter Cookies recipe (page 193) just before adding the flour in step 1. Continue with the recipe from step 2.

COOKIES

SPICED MAPLE

Add 1 tsp ground mixed spice (apple pie spice) to 1 quantity Basic Vanilla Butter Cookies recipe (page 193) when adding the flour in step 1. Continue with the recipe from step 2. To make maple icing, combine ¾ cup (90g) sifted icing (confectioners') sugar, 1½ tbsp maple syrup and 3 tsp water; beat with a wooden spoon until icing is smooth and a pouring consistency. Drizzle icing on top of cooled cookies.

4 WAYS

LEMON & CRANBERRY

Add 1 tsp finely grated lemon zest and ½ cup (65g) dried cranberries to 1 quantity Basic Vanilla Butter Cookies recipe (page 193) just before adding the flour in step 1. Continue with the recipe from step 2.

TRIPLE-CHOC COOKIES

ORANGE & PECAN COOKIES

LEMON & CRANBERRY COOKIES

SPICED MAPLE COOKIES

CHOCOLATE LAVA CAKES

25g (¾oz) butter, softened, plus
   125g (4oz) extra, chopped
2 tbsp unsweetened cocoa powder
155g (5oz) dark (semi-sweet)
   chocolate, coarsely chopped
2 eggs
2 egg yolks
⅓ cup (75g) caster (superfine) sugar
¼ cup (35g) plain (all-purpose) flour
to serve: extra cocoa powder, to
   dust, and coffee ice cream

1 Grease six ¾-cup (180ml) ovenproof dishes (ramekins or metal dariole moulds) with the 25g (¾oz) softened butter; dust with cocoa, shaking off excess.
2 Stir chocolate and the extra 125g (4oz) chopped butter in a small saucepan over a low heat until smooth. Allow to cool for 10 minutes. Transfer mixture to a large bowl.
3 Beat eggs, egg yolks and sugar in a small bowl with an electric mixer until thick and creamy. Fold egg mixture and sifted flour into barely warm chocolate mixture. Spoon mixture into dishes.
4 Preheat a 7-litre air fryer to 180°C/350°F for 3 minutes.
5 Taking care, place dishes in the air-fryer basket; at 180°C/350°F, cook for 10–12 minutes. Remove from the basket. Leave cakes in the dishes for 1 minute before gently inverting onto serving plates.
6 Dust cakes with extra cocoa and serve immediately with ice cream.

TIPS These cakes should be served shortly after they come out of the air fryer. If they are allowed to sit for longer than 1 minute, the gooey centre will firm up and the chocolate won't ooze out when they're cut. Warning: the melted chocolate centre will be hot, so take care when biting into the cake.

**prep + cook time
30 minutes (+ cooling)
serves 6**

CHOCOLATE CANNOLI
WITH HAZELNUT CREAM

1 cup (150g) plain (all-purpose) flour
1 tbsp cocoa powder
1 tbsp caster (superfine) sugar
1 egg
1 egg yolk
1 tbsp Marsala
2 tsp olive oil
2 tsp cold water
1 egg white, lightly beaten
olive oil cooking spray
to serve: icing (confectioners') sugar
    and fresh raspberries

HAZELNUT CREAM
1 cup (250ml) double (heavy) cream
2 tbsp icing (confectioners') sugar
125g (4oz) mascarpone
¼ cup (85g) hazelnut chocolate
    spread

1 Process flour, cocoa and sugar until just combined. Add egg, egg yolk, Marsala, oil and the 2 tablespoons cold water; process until dough starts to come together. Turn out onto a lightly floured surface; knead until smooth. Divide dough in half and shape into two discs; wrap in cling film. Refrigerate for 1 hour.

2 Roll out one dough disc on a lightly floured surface until 2mm thick (alternatively, roll dough through a pasta machine). Using a 10cm (4in) round cutter, cut out six rounds, re-rolling the scraps if necessary. Wrap each round around an ungreased metal cannoli mould (see tip), overlapping ends slightly. Brush ends with a little egg white to secure (ensure you don't get egg white on the moulds; otherwise the dough will stick to them once cooked). Repeat with remaining dough disc to make 12 cannoli shells in total.

3 Preheat a 7-litre air fryer to 200°C/400°F for 3 minutes.

4 Spray cannoli all over with oil. Taking care, line the air-fryer basket with baking parchment. Place cannoli in the basket; at 200°C/400°F, cook for 7 minutes, turning halfway through cooking time, or until golden. Using tongs, transfer to a plate to cool slightly. Carefully remove moulds from warm cannoli. Allow to cool.

5 Meanwhile, to make hazelnut cream, beat cream and icing sugar in a small bowl with an electric mixer until soft peaks form. Add mascarpone and hazelnut chocolate spread; beat for 20 seconds or until just combined. Spoon cream mixture into a piping bag fitted with a 1cm (½in) plain nozzle. Pipe hazelnut cream into cooled cannoli shells.

6 Dust cannoli with icing sugar. Serve with raspberries.

TIP Cannelloni pasta shells can be used instead of speciality metal cannoli moulds; however, you will need to grease them first. Ensure that you wrap the dough rounds loosely around the pasta shells, to make removing them easier.

prep + cook time
45 minutes
(+ refrigeration) makes 12

KEEP IT Tart will
keep in an airtight
container in the fridge
for up to 3 days.

TANGY LEMON TART

125g (4oz) butter, coarsely chopped
¼ cup (40g) icing (confectioners')
   sugar
1¼ cups (185g) plain
   (all-purpose) flour
3 eggs
1 cup (220g) caster (superfine)
   sugar, plus 2 tbsp extra
2 tsp finely grated lemon zest
½ cup (125ml) lemon juice
cooking oil spray
1 medium lemon (140g), thinly sliced
to serve: extra icing (confectioners')
   sugar, to dust

1 Preheat a 5.3-litre air fryer to 180°C/350°F for 3 minutes. Grease a 20cm (8in) loose-bottomed tart tin.

2 Beat butter and icing sugar in a small bowl with an electric mixer until smooth. Stir in 1 cup (150g) of the flour until a dough forms. Press mixture evenly over bottom and up the side of tart tin. Fold a length of foil into a long strip; place under tart tin to act as a sling.

3 Taking care, lower tart tin, on the sling, into the air-fryer basket; at 180°C/350°F, cook for 10 minutes.

4 Using the back of a spoon, press crust back down over the bottom and up the side of tart tin; cook for a further 8 minutes until tart base is dry and lightly golden.

5 Meanwhile, to make lemon filling, place eggs, the 1 cup (220g) caster sugar, remaining flour, the lemon zest and juice in a medium saucepan; whisk continuously over a medium heat until mixture boils and thickens.

6 Pour hot filling mixture into a jug; pour over the hot tart base in the basket. Reset the temperature to 160°C/325°F; cook for 3–5 minutes until filling is set. Using the foil sling as an aid, lift from the basket and place on a wire rack. Leave tart in tin to cool.

7 Meanwhile, spray the basket with oil. Sprinkle lemon slices with the extra 2 tablespoons caster sugar and place in the basket; at 160°C/325°F, cook for 6 minutes until caramelized.

8 To serve, top tart with caramelized lemon slices and dust with extra icing sugar.

**prep + cook time
45 minutes serves 8**

MEGA CARROT CAKE MUFFINS

2 cups (240g) ground almonds
2 tbsp chia seeds
1 tsp baking powder (see tip)
½ tsp bicarbonate of soda
   (baking soda)
1 tsp ground cinnamon
1 tbsp ground ginger
3 eggs
¼ cup (60ml) extra virgin olive oil
¾ cup (110g) coconut sugar
2 tsp vanilla extract
1 large courgette (zucchini) (150g)
1 large carrot (180g)
1 large apple (200g)
½ cup (120g) smooth ricotta
¼ cup (40g) natural almonds,
   chopped

1 Preheat a 5.3-litre air fryer to 160°C/325°F for 3 minutes. Triple-layer 18 muffin wraps to make six thick wraps.
2 Combine ground almonds, chia seeds, baking powder, bicarbonate of soda and spices in a large bowl. Whisk eggs, oil, coconut sugar and vanilla in a medium bowl; add to dry ingredients, stirring until just combined.
3 Coarsely grate courgette, carrot and apple into a medium bowl. Using your hands, pick up handfuls of the courgette mixture and squeeze very firmly to remove excess liquid. Fold courgette mixture into almond mixture until just combined. Divide muffin mixture evenly among muffin wraps.
4 Taking care, place muffin wraps in the air-fryer basket; at 160°C/325°F, cook for 5 minutes.

5 Cover top of muffins with a piece of foil; cook for a further 25 minutes.
6 Top each muffin with a spoonful of ricotta and scatter with chopped almonds; at 160°C/325°F, cook for 5 minutes until ricotta is browned and a skewer inserted into the centre of a muffin comes out clean. Transfer to a wire rack to cool.

KEEP IT Muffins will keep in an airtight container in the fridge for up to 1 week, or they can be frozen for up to 2 months.

TIP To make gluten-free muffins, use a gluten-free brand of baking powder.

**prep + cook time
45 minutes makes 6**

LEMON CURD & RASPBERRY
BREAD & BUTTER PUDDING

250g (8oz) crusty sourdough bread, thickly sliced
½ cup (160g) ready-made lemon curd
1 cup (250ml) double (heavy) cream
¾ cup (180ml) milk
3 eggs
¼ cup (55g) caster (superfine) sugar
1 tsp vanilla extract
125g (4oz) frozen raspberries
to serve: extra lemon curd

1 Grease a 1.5-litre (6-cup), 20cm (8in) round baking dish; ensure the dish will fit into a 7-litre air fryer.
2 Spread bread slices thickly with lemon curd. Arrange bread, curd-side up, in dish.
3 To make custard, combine cream and milk in a microwave-safe jug; heat in microwave on HIGH (100%) for 2 minutes or until warm. Whisk eggs, sugar and vanilla in a bowl until combined; gradually whisk in warm cream mixture until combined.
4 Pour custard over bread slices in dish; scatter with raspberries. Using a spatula, press bread down gently to submerge in the custard. Allow to stand for 5 minutes. Cover dish tightly with foil.

5 Preheat air fryer to 150°C/300°F for 5 minutes.
6 Taking care, place dish in the air-fryer basket; at 150°C/300°F, cook for 30 minutes.
7 Remove foil. Reset the temperature to 160°C/325°F; cook for a further 12 minutes until golden and just set. Remove from the basket. Allow pudding to stand for 5 minutes to cool slightly.
8 Serve pudding dolloped with extra lemon curd.

**prep + cook time
1 hour serves 12**

TIP Homemade pesto
can be replaced with
¼ cup (65g) bottled
basil or sun-dried
tomato pesto.

CHEESY PESTO SCROLLS

1 cup (50g) firmly packed
   basil leaves
1 garlic clove, chopped
2 tbsp pine nuts, toasted
2 tbsp finely grated Parmesan
¼ cup (60ml) extra virgin olive oil
1 tbsp lemon juice
2 cups (300g) self-raising flour
1 tsp fine salt
1 tbsp caster (superfine) sugar
50g (1½oz) cold butter,
   coarsely chopped
about ¾ cup (180ml) milk

CHEESY FILLING
½ cup (60g) grated mozzarella
¼ cup (35g) grated Cheddar
¼ cup (25g) grated Parmesan

1 To make pesto, process basil, garlic, pine nuts and Parmesan in a food processor until chopped finely. With motor operating, gradually add combined oil and lemon juice until pesto is almost smooth; season with salt and freshly ground black pepper.

2 Sift flour and salt into a medium bowl; stir in sugar. Using your fingers, rub in butter. Add enough milk to form a soft, sticky dough. Turn out onto a lightly floured sheet of baking parchment; lightly knead until smooth. Sprinkle parchment with more flour, if needed. Roll out dough into a 30cm x 40cm (12in x 16in) rectangle.

3 Spread dough evenly with the pesto. Scatter cheeses for filling evenly over pesto. Roll up dough tightly from a long side to form a log; place log in the freezer for 10 minutes to firm slightly.

4 Preheat a 7-litre air fryer to 160°C/325°F for 5 minutes.

5 Using a serrated knife, trim ends off the log; cut into 12 slices.

6 Taking care, line the air-fryer basket with baking parchment. Place scrolls, cut-side up, in the basket, then cover basket tightly with foil; at 160°C/325°F, cook for 10 minutes.

7 Remove foil; cook for a further 10 minutes until scrolls are golden and cooked through.

8 Serve scrolls warm or cold.

prep + cook time
50 minutes (+ freezing)
makes 12

PASSION FRUIT BUTTERMILK CAKE

125g (4oz) butter
1 cup (220g) caster (superfine) sugar
2 tsp vanilla extract
2 eggs
2 cups (300g) self-raising flour
⅔ cup (160ml) buttermilk
¾ cup (180ml) passion fruit pulp (see tip)
1½ cups (240g) icing (confectioners') sugar

1 Preheat a 7-litre air fryer to 160°C/325°F for 5 minutes. Grease a deep 20cm (8in) round springform cake tin; line bottom and side of tin with baking parchment. Ensure that the tin will fit into the air fryer.

2 Beat butter, caster sugar and vanilla in a bowl with an electric mixer until thick and creamy. Beat in eggs, one at a time, until combined. Fold in flour, buttermilk and ¼ cup (60ml) of the passion fruit pulp. Spoon mixture into cake tin; cover with foil.

3 Taking care, place cake tin in the air-fryer basket; at 160°C/325°F, cook for 30 minutes.

4 Remove foil; cook for a further 30 minutes or until a skewer inserted into the centre comes out clean. Remove from the basket. Leave cake in tin for 10 minutes before turning out onto a wire rack to cool.

5 To make passion fruit icing, combine icing sugar and remaining passion fruit pulp in a small bowl. Spread top of cooled cake with icing.

TIP You will need about 9 passion fruit for this recipe.

prep + cook time 1¼ hours (+ cooling) serves 12

BANANA FRITTERS
WITH SALTED CARAMEL SAUCE

15g (½oz) butter, chopped
1½ cups (110g) panko breadcrumbs
½ cup (40g) desiccated (shredded)
   coconut
½ cup (75g) plain (all-purpose) flour
2 eggs
¼ cup (60ml) milk
4 ripe bananas, halved lengthways
to serve: vanilla ice cream

SALTED CARAMEL SAUCE
½ cup (125ml) double (heavy) cream
½ cup (110g) firmly packed light
   soft brown sugar
30g (1oz) butter, chopped
1 tsp sea salt flakes

1 Melt butter in a medium frying pan over a medium-high heat. Add breadcrumbs and coconut; cook, stirring, for 2 minutes or until breadcrumbs are lightly browned. Transfer to a plate to cool.
2 Place flour on a plate. Whisk eggs and milk together in a medium shallow bowl. Dust bananas in flour, shaking off excess, dip in egg mixture, then coat in breadcrumb mixture. Refrigerate for 15 minutes.
3 Preheat a 7-litre air fryer to 180°C/350°F for 3 minutes.
4 Taking care, place fritters in the air-fryer basket; at 180°C/350°F, cook for 8 minutes, turning halfway through cooking time, or until golden.
5 Meanwhile, to make salted caramel sauce, stir ingredients, except salt, in a small saucepan over a low heat, without boiling, until sugar dissolves. Bring to the boil, then reduce heat; simmer for 3 minutes or until slightly thickened. Remove from heat and stir in salt.
6 Serve fritters with ice cream, drizzled with salted caramel sauce.

**prep + cook time
25 minutes
(+ refrigeration)
serves 4**

211

BANANA BREAD

125g (4oz) butter, softened
1 cup (220g) firmly packed light soft
   brown sugar
1 tsp vanilla extract
2 eggs
1½ cups (350g) mashed ripe banana
   (see tip)
¼ cup (60ml) maple syrup
1⅔ cups (250g) plain
   (all-purpose) flour
1 tsp baking powder
1 tsp bicarbonate of soda
   (baking soda)
1½ tsp ground cinnamon
¼ tsp sea salt flakes
½ cup (25g) coarsely chopped
   roasted walnuts
2 small bananas (130g each),
   halved lengthways
2 tbsp demerara (raw) sugar
to serve: soft ricotta and honey

1 Grease a 10.5cm x 20cm (4in x 8in) loaf tin; line bottom and sides with baking parchment, ensuring parchment sits flush with the rim.
2 Beat butter, brown sugar and vanilla in a medium bowl with an electric mixer until pale and fluffy. Beat in eggs, one at a time, until just combined, then mashed banana and maple syrup. Sift over flour, baking powder, bicarbonate of soda, cinnamon and salt. Add walnuts; stir with a large spoon until combined. Spoon mixture into loaf tin; smooth surface.
3 Preheat a 5.3-litre air fryer to 160°C/325°F for 3 minutes.
4 Taking care, place loaf tin in the air-fryer basket; at 160°C/325°F, cook for 10 minutes.

5 Place banana halves, cut-side up, on top of bread. Cover loaf tin with foil and pierce the foil; at 160°C/325°F, cook for 40 minutes.
6 Remove foil; cook for another 5 minutes until a skewer inserted into the centre comes out clean. Remove from the basket. Leave bread in tin for 10 minutes before turning out, top-side up, onto a wire rack to cool. Sprinkle top with demerara sugar while hot.
7 Serve slices of banana bread topped with ricotta and drizzled with honey.

TIP You will need 3 large bananas to make 1½ cups mashed banana.

prep + cook time
1¼ hours serves 8

BERRY BAKED PANCAKE

olive oil cooking spray
1 cup (150g) plain (all-purpose) flour
¼ cup (55g) caster (superfine) sugar
¼ tsp bicarbonate of soda
   (baking soda)
⅔ cup (160ml) buttermilk
1 egg, lightly beaten
2 tsp vanilla extract
30g (1oz) butter, melted
50g (1½oz) blueberries
50g (1½oz) raspberries
to serve: icing (confectioners') sugar
   and maple syrup

1 Preheat a 7-litre air fryer to 180°C/350°F for 3 minutes. Spray a non-stick 18cm (7¼in) round, 2.5cm (1in) deep pizza pan (see tip) with oil.
2 Place flour, sugar and bicarbonate of soda in a large bowl; stir to combine. Whisk buttermilk, egg, vanilla and butter in a medium jug or bowl. Add buttermilk mixture to flour mixture, stirring until just combined. Spread mixture into pizza pan and smooth top; scatter with berries, pressing them in gently.

3 Taking care, place pizza pan in the air-fryer basket; at 180°C/350°F, cook for 15 minutes until a skewer inserted into the centre comes out clean.
4 Dust warm pancake with icing sugar and serve with maple syrup.

TIP Many air fryers come with an accessory pack that includes a pizza pan.

**prep + cook time
30 minutes serves 4**

215

COOKIE PIE

220g (7oz) frozen shortcrust
   pastry case
75g (2½oz) butter, softened
⅔ cup (150g) firmly packed
   light soft brown sugar
1 egg
1 tsp vanilla extract
1 cup (150g) self-raising flour
pinch of salt
¼ cup (45g) dark (semi-sweet)
   chocolate chips
¾ cup (110g) assorted chocolates
   (see tip)
to serve: icing (confectioners') sugar

1 Preheat a 5.3-litre air fryer to 170°C/340°F for 3 minutes.

2 Cover frozen pastry case with foil, then weigh foil down with two metal spoons. Taking care, place pastry case in the air-fryer basket; at 170°C/340°F, cook for 10 minutes until pastry is lightly golden and dry. Transfer to a chopping board to cool.

3 Meanwhile, to make chocolate chip cookie filling, beat butter, sugar, egg and vanilla in a small bowl with an electric mixer for 6 minutes or until light and creamy. Stir in sifted flour and salt, then chocolate chips.

4 Fill pastry case with the filling; smooth surface. Press assorted chocolates and sweets (candies) into top of pie. Place pie in the basket; cover with foil.

5 Reset the temperature to 160°C/325°F; cook for 30 minutes until a skewer inserted into the centre of the pie comes out with a few crumbs attached and top is browned and puffed.

6 Serve pie warm or cool, dusted with icing sugar.

TIP For pie one (top left) we used Smarties, Rolos (caramel-filled chocolate rolls) and chocolate nonpareils (chocolate freckles or jazzies). For pie two (top right) we used sliced liquorice allsorts, Rolos, unicorn confetti and strawberry-flavoured Pocky sticks. For pie three (bottom) we used Smarties, Rolos, chocolate-coated pretzels, cake decorations and mini letter cookies. Fire up your imagination and get creative with confectionery.

SERVE IT Serve with scoops of vanilla ice cream.

prep + cook time 1 hour
makes 1 pie (serves 6)

MUESLI BARS

2 cups (180g) rolled oats
⅓ cup (50g) sunflower seeds
¼ cup (50g) pepitas (pumpkin
  seed kernels)
125g (4oz) dried apricots
2 tbsp white chia seeds
2 tbsp boiling water
⅓ cup (25g) desiccated coconut
100g (3oz) butter, chopped
⅓ cup (75g) firmly packed brown
  sugar
2 tbsp honey
½ tsp ground cinnamon

1 Process 1 cup (90g) oats until the consistency of desiccated coconut. Add sunflower seeds and pepitas; pulse briefly until a few are coarsely chopped. Transfer mixture to a large bowl. Process apricots, chia seeds and the boiling water until finely chopped; add to the bowl with coconut.

2 Stir butter, sugar, honey and cinnamon in a medium saucepan over low heat until sugar dissolves and mixture is smooth; stir into oat mixture until combined, then stir in remaining oats.

3 Remove the basket from the pan of a 5.3-litre air fryer and place on a sheet of baking paper; trace around the base. Cut out shape 2cm (¾in) larger than the marked tracing. Grease basket and line with the paper cut-out.

4 Press oat mixture very firmly over the paper; use the base of a glass or an offset spatula to compact the mixture. Insert the basket back into the air fryer pan; at 140°C/285°F, cook for 40 minutes.

5 Remove the basket from the air fryer pan and place on a wire rack to cool completely. Using the paper as an aid, lift the slice from the basket and transfer to a board; cut into 12 bars.

KEEP IT Muesli bars will keep in an airtight container for up to 2 weeks.

prep + cook time 1 hour makes 12

CONVERSION CHART

MEASURES

One Australian metric measuring cup holds approximately 250ml; one Australian metric tablespoon holds 20ml; one Australian metric teaspoon holds 5ml. North America, New Zealand and the United Kingdom use a 15ml tablespoon.

The difference between one country's measuring cups and another's is within a two- or three-teaspoon variance and will not affect your cooking results. All cup and spoon measurements are level.

The most accurate way of measuring dry ingredients is to weigh them.

When measuring liquids, use a clear glass or plastic jug with metric markings.We use extra-large eggs with an average weight of 60g each.

DRY MEASURES

metric	imperial
15g	½oz
30g	1oz
60g	2oz
90g	3oz
125g	4oz (¼lb)
155g	5oz
185g	6oz
220g	7oz
250g	8oz (½lb)
280g	9oz
315g	10oz
345g	11oz
375g	12oz (¾lb)
410g	13oz
440g	14oz
470g	15oz
500g	16oz (1lb)
750g	24oz (1½lb)
1kg	32oz (2lb)

LIQUID MEASURES

metric	imperial
30ml	1 fluid oz
60ml	2 fluid oz
100ml	3 fluid oz
125ml	4 fluid oz
150ml	5 fluid oz
190ml	6 fluid oz
250ml	8 fluid oz
300ml	10 fluid oz
500ml	16 fluid oz
600ml	20 fluid oz
1000ml (1 litre)	1¾ pints

LENGTH MEASURES

metric	imperial
3mm	⅛in
6mm	¼in
1cm	½in
2cm	¾in
2.5cm	1in
5cm	2in
6cm	2½in
8cm	3in
10cm	4in
13cm	5in
15cm	6in
18cm	7in
20cm	8in
22cm	9in
25cm	10in
28cm	11in
30cm	12in (1ft)

OVEN TEMPERATURES

The oven temperatures below are for conventional ovens; if you are using a fan-forced oven, reduce the temperature by 20 degrees.

	°C (Celsius)	°F (Fahrenheit)
Very slow	120	250
Slow	150	300
Moderately slow	160	325
Moderate	180	350
Moderately hot	200	400
Hot	220	425
Very hot	240	475

Measurements for cake tins are approximate only. Using same-shaped cake tins of a similar size should not affect the outcome of your baking. We measure the inside top of the cake tin to determine size.

INDEX

A

almonds
  berry frangipane galette 188
  mega carrot cake muffins 202
apples
  appley pie rolls 190
  dried apple 37
apricot & pistachio stuffed leg
  of lamb 160
Asian salad 164
asparagus with prosciutto 113
aubergine
  aubergine & ricotta pizza 60
  aubergine parmigiana "meatball"
    subs 147
  stuffed aubergine with lentils 66
avocados
  avocado salsa 68
  miso avocado dressing 74

B

bacon
  bacon & leek frittatas 33
  bacon 'n' cheese burgers 46
  cheesy bacon pull-apart 154
  feta, dill & bacon potatoes 145
  mini meatloaves wrapped in
    maple bacom 132
  pizza 60
bananas
  banana bread 212
  banana fritters 211
barbecue bourbon chicken
  wings 59
beans
  cheat's sausage cassoulet 171
  crispy pepperoni-flavoured peas
    & beans 30
  epic jacket potatoes 121
  white bean shakshuka 163
Béarnaise sauce 130
beef
  bacon 'n' cheese burgers 46
  beef skewers 50
  classic meatballs 80
  herb-crusted roast beef 140–41
  loaded Korean burger 87
  Mexican stuffed meatballs 80
  mini meatloaves wrapped in
    maple bacon 132
  steak with Béarnaise & fries 130–31
beetroot
  beetroot with yogurt & dukkah 118
  veggie chips 41
berry baked pancake 215
berry frangipane galette 188

bread
  basic dough 155
  cheesy bacon pull-apart 154
  cheesy pesto scrolls 207
  garlic & Parmesan twist 154
  mixed-seed buns 154
  spiced prawn po' boys 79
  tomato pesto focaccia 154
bread & butter pudding 204
broccoli
  Brussels sprouts revolution 101
  crisp tofu with palm sugar
    dressing 126
  sesame & chilli broccolini with
    mushrooms 122
brownies, peanut butter 183
Brussels sprouts revolution 101
buns, mixed seed 154
burgers 46, 87
butter cookies, basic vanilla 193
butterflied harissa chicken 138

C

cabbage
  kimchi slaw 87
  vegetable spring rolls 23
Cajun sweet potato wedges 92
cakes
  banana bread 212
  chocolate cake 176
  chocolate lava cakes 197
  passion fruit buttermilk cake 208
  peanut butter brownies 183
calzones, pepperoni 72
caramel
  salted caramel sauce 211
carrots
  carrot koshimbir 142
  maple-roasted carrots 95
  mega carrot cake muffins 202
  Parmesan, thyme & carrot rösti 125
  veggie chips 41
cassoulet, cheat's sausage 171
cauliflower filo triangles 14
cheese
  bacon 'n' cheese burgers 46
  cauliflower filo triangles 14
  cheesy bacon pull-apart 154
  cheesy pesto scrolls 207
  chicken chimichangas 68
  chicken parmigiana 168
  courgette balls 29
  feta, dill & bacon potatoes 145
  feta dressing 74
  garlic & Parmesan twist 154
  Greek feta & oregano fries 26

Halloumi fries 26
herb baked ricotta 21
kale, pear, smoked Cheddar
  & almond salad 98
loaded sweetcorn 110
loaded Korean burger 87
Mexican stuffed meatballs 80
Parmesan, thyme & carrot rösti 125
pear & ricotta fritters 42
pizza 60
potato gratin 109
roasted squash 107
spinach & feta twists 38
stuffed aubergine with lentils 66
sun-dried tomato & feta chips 18
sweet potato parmigiana 49
veggie mac 'n' cheese
  croquettes 104
chicken
  barbecue bourbon chicken wings 59
  butterflied harissa chicken 138
  chicken & leek pie 136
  chicken chimichangas 68
  chicken parmigiana 168
  chicken wings 65
  crumbed chicken 83
  green curry chicken 167
  Italian chicken rissoles 76
  lemon & garlic roast chicken 84
  Portuguese chicken drumsticks 88
  Southern fried chicken 172–3
  green falafel 17
chickpeas
  crispy pepperoni-flavoured peas
    & beans 30
chillies
  chilli & lime mayo 75
  chilli garlic fries 117
  chilli peanut dressing 75
  sesame & chilli broccolini with
    mushrooms 122
chimichurri 75
chips & fries 7
  Cajun sweet potato wedges 92
  chilli garlic fries 117
  courgette fries 26
  Greek feta & oregano fries 26
  Halloumi fries 26
  lemon pepper fries 117
  paprika potato wedges 117
  pickle chips 24
  salted fries 117
  spicy Cajun potato wedges 117
  steak with Béarnaise & fries 130–31
  sun-dried tomato & feta chips 18
  sweet potato wedges 117
  veggie chips 41
chive butter 114

chocolate
  chocolate cake 176
  chocolate cannoli 198
  chocolate lava cakes 197
  churros with chocolate sauce 179
  cookie pie 216
  peanut butter brownies 183
  triple-choc cookies 194
chorizo pizza 60
churros with chocolate sauce 179
coconut honey prawns 54
cookie pie 216
cookies
  basic vanilla butter cookies 193
  triple-choc cookies 194
  spiced maple cookies 194
  orange & pecan cookies 194
  lemon & cranberry cookies 194
courgette
  veggie mac 'n' cheese
    croquettes 104
  courgette balls 29
  courgette fries 26
cranberries
  lemon & cranberry cookies 194
crispy pepperoni-flavoured peas
  & beans 30
curry 62, 167

D
dehydrated snacks 37
dips 21, 24, 26
dressings 74–5

E
edamame
  crispy pepperoni-flavoured peas
    & beans 30
  edamame slaw 98
  green falafel 17
eggs
  bacon & leek frittatas 33
  white bean shakshuka 163

F
falafel, green 17
fishcakes, salmon 62
fish tacos, Jamaican 53
focaccia, tomato pesto 154
frangipane galette 188
fries see chips & fries
frittatas, bacon & leek 33
fritters 42, 102, 179, 211
fudge icing 176

G
garlic
  chilli garlic fries 117
  chimichurri 75
  garlic & Parmesan twist 154
  lemon & garlic roast chicken 84
Greek-style potatoes 145
Greek yogurt dipping sauce 26

H
Halloumi fries 26
harissa chicken 138
hash browns 152
hasselback sweet potatoes 114–15
hazelnut cream 198
hoisin pork 159
honey sauce 54

I
icing, fudge 176
Italian chicken rissoles 76
Italian-style rice salad 98

J
Jamaican fish tacos 53
Japanese salmon 156–7

K
kale, pear, smoked Cheddar & almond
  salad 98
kimchi slaw 87
kiwi fruit, dried 37
koftas, herby lamb 57

L
lamb
  apricot & pistachio stuffed leg 160
  Greek lamb meatballs 80
  herby lamb koftas 57
  tikka lamb cutlets 142
leeks
  bacon & leek frittatas 33
  chicken & leek pie 136
lemon
  lemon & cranberry cookies 194
  lemon & garlic roast chicken 84
  lemon & herb pork schnitzels 148
  lemon curd & raspberry bread
    & butter pudding 204
  lemon curd scones 180
  lemon pepper fries 117
  tangy lemon tart 201
lentils
  lentil tabbouleh 98
  stuffed aubergine with lentils 66

M
mac 'n' cheese croquettes 104
maple syrup
  maple-roasted carrots 95
  mini meatloaves wrapped
    in maple bacon 132
  spiced maple cookies 194
mayonnaise
  chilli & lime 75
  spicy 83
meatballs 57, 80, 147
meatloaves, mini 132
Mexican stuffed meatballs 80
miso avocado dressing 74
miso sauce 156–7
muesli bars 218
muffins, mega carrot cake 202
mushrooms
  creamy mushrooms 140–41
  sesame & chilli broccolini with
    mushrooms 122
mustard & mint potatoes 145

O
olives
  green olive dressing 74
onion rings, golden 102
orange & pecan cookies 194

P
palm sugar dressing 126
pancake, berry baked 215
paprika potato wedges 117
parsley
  chimichurri 75
  salsa verde 18
parsnip
  veggie chips 41
passion fruit buttermilk cake 208
pastries 14, 38, 72, 184–90, 198
peanut butter
  peanut butter brownies 183
  spicy Korean peanut pork ribs 135
peanuts
  chilli peanut dressing 75
  peanut rice 159
pears
  kale, pear, smoked Cheddar
    & almond salad 98
  pear & ricotta fritters 42
pecans
  orange & pecan cookies 194
pepita salsa 107
pepperoni calzones 72
peppers
  beef skewers 50
  cheat's sausage cassoulet 171
  pepperoni calzones 72

white bean shakshuka 163
peri-peri potatoes 145
pesto
  cheesy pesto scrolls 207
  tomato pesto focaccia 154
pickle chips 24
pickled radish 167
pies 136, 216
pineapple
  dried pineapple 37
  pineapple huli huli chicken wings 65
pizzas 60
polenta
  sun-dried tomato & feta chips 18
pomegranate chicken wings 65
pop tarts, strawberry 186
pork
  caramelized onion, dill & caraway
    sausage rolls 184
  cracking pork belly & Asian
    salad 164
  hoisin pork 159
  lemon & herb pork schnitzels 148
  ridiculously good ribs 151
  spicy Korean peanut pork ribs 135
Portuguese chicken drumsticks 88
potatoes
  epic jacket potatoes 121
  feta, dill & bacon potatoes 145
  Greek-style potatoes 145
  lemon pepper fries 117
  mustard & mint potatoes 145
  paprika potato wedges 117
  Parmesan, thyme & carrot rösti 125
  peri-peri potatoes 145
  potato gratin 109
  roast potatoes 160
  salmon fishcakes 62
  salt 'n' vinegar smashed potatoes 97
  salted fries 117
  spicy Cajun potato wedges 117
  steak with Béarnaise & fries 130–31
prawns
  coconut honey prawns 54
  prawn pizza 60
  spiced prawn po' boys 79
prosciutto
  asparagus with 113
  Italian chicken rissoles 76

R

radish, pickled 167
ranch dipping sauce 24
raspberries
  lemon curd & raspberry bread
    & butter pudding 204
red cabbage
  edamame slaw 98
rice
  Italian-style rice salad 98
  peanut rice 159

rissoles 76
rösti 125

S

salads 57, 98, 164
salmon
  crisp-skinned salmon 71
  Japanese salmon 156–7
  salmon fishcakes 62
salsas 18, 68, 71, 107
salt 'n' vinegar smashed potatoes 97
salted caramel sauce 211
salted fries 117
sauces 74–5
sausage rolls 184
sausages
  cheat's sausage cassoulet 171
  corn & sweet potato hash
    browns 152
scones, lemon curd 180
seeds
  mixed-seed buns 154
  pepita salsa 107
sesame seeds
  sesame & chilli broccolini
    with mushrooms 122
  sticky sesame chicken wings 65
shakshuka, white bean 163
slaw 87, 98
Southern fried chicken 172–3
spinach
  Asian salad 164
  green tahini 101
  pepperoni calzones 72
  spinach & feta twists 38
spring rolls, vegetable 23
squash, roasted 107
sriracha & lime butter 110
sriracha vegetable tempura 34
steak with Béarnaise & fries 130–31
strawberry pop tarts 186
sun-dried tomato & feta chips 18
sweetcorn
  loaded sweetcorn 110
  sweetcorn & sweet potato
    hash browns 152
sweet potatoes
  Cajun sweet potato wedges 92
  corn & sweet potato hash
    browns 152
  hasselback sweet potatoes 114–15
  sweet potato parmigiana 49
  sweet potato wedges 117

T

tabbouleh 98
tacos, Jamaican fish 53
tahini
  green tahini 57, 101

tahini sauce 17
tarts 188, 201
tempura, sriracha vegetable 34
tikka lamb cutlets 142
tofu
  crisp tofu with palm sugar
    dressing 126
tomatoes
  chicken parmigiana 168–9
  classic meatballs 80
  stuffed aubergine with lentils 66
  sun-dried tomato & feta chips 18
  tomato pesto focaccia 154
  tomato salad 57
tortillas
  chicken chimichangas 68
  Jamaican fish tacos 53
tzatziki, garlic 50

V

vegetable spring rolls 23
veggie chips 41
veggie dippers 21
veggie mac 'n' cheese croquettes 104

W

watermelon, dried 37
wedges see chips & fries

Y

yogurt
  beetroot with yogurt & dukkah 118
  Greek yogurt dipping sauce 26
  green tahini 57
  lemon yogurt 29
  tahini sauce 17

ACKNOWLEDGMENTS

DK would like to thank John Friend for
proofreading, Hilary Bird for indexing,
and Sophia Young, Joe Revill, Amanda
Chebatte, and Georgia Moore for their
assistance in making this book.

The Australian Women's Weekly Test
Kitchen in Sydney has developed,
tested, and photographed the recipes
in this book.

Project Editor Siobhán O'Connor
DTP and Design Coordinator Heather Blagden
Jacket Designer Maxine Pedliham
Jacket Coordinator Jasmin Lennie
Senior Production Editor Tony Phipps
Senior Production Controller Stephanie McConnell
Editorial Director Cara Armstrong
Art Director Maxine Pedliham
Publishing Director Katie Cowan

DK DELHI
Managing Art Editor Neha Ahuja
DTP Coordinator Pushpak Tyagi
DTP Designers Raman Panwar, Satish Gaur
Pre-production Manager Balwant Singh

First published in Great Britain in 2023 by
Dorling Kindersley Limited
DK, One Embassy Gardens, 8 Viaduct Gardens,
London, SW11 7BW

The authorized representative in the EEA is
Dorling Kindersley Verlag GmbH. Arnulfstr. 124,
80636 Munich, Germany

Copyright © 2023 Dorling Kindersley Limited
A Penguin Random House Company
15 14 13 12 11 10 9 8 7
010–338489–Apr/2023

A CIP catalogue record for this book
is available from the British Library.
ISBN: 978-0-2416-4902-2

Printed and bound in China

www.dk.com

MIX
Paper | Supporting
responsible forestry
FSC™ C018179

This book was made with Forest
Stewardship Council™ certified
paper – one small step in DK's
commitment to a sustainable future.
Learn more at **www.dk.com/uk/
information/sustainability**